ACCIDENTALS

ACCIDENTALS

Lawrence Sail

illustrations by Erica Sail

Published 2020 by Impress Books.

Cover design by BMLD.

Printed and bound in England.

A catalogue record for this book is available from the British Library.

ISBN: 978-1-911293-51-4

Contents

Contents

Illustrations

for Helen, Grace and Rose

Acknowledgements

I would like to thank all those who have generously given me help along the way, especially: Michael and Simone Bird, for the use of the flat in Berlin; Hubert Moore and Jane Champion, for introducing me to the bluebell wood; Bloodaxe Books, for permission to include poems originally published by them – 'Calm Sea at Night', 'Fish Magic' and 'Anchor' in *Waking Dreams: New & Selected Poems* (2010), 'From the Lighthouse' in *The Quick* (2015), 'Heartsong', 'Sea Pictures', 'Sarabande' and 'The Smoke-tree' in *Guises* (2020); Lachlan Mackinnon for permission to use lines from his poem 'Nocturne' (in *Doves*, Faber 2017); and the estate of Michael Hamburger for the use of lines from his translation of Goethe's poem 'Vom Vater hab' ich die Statur'. Thanks are also due to Graham Davies; Richard Willis and his colleagues at Impress Books; and Jeff Collyer.

'The principle which controls it is simply that it should give pleasure; the desire which impels us when we take it from the shelf is simply to receive pleasure.'

VIRGINIA WOOLF, 'The Modern Essay'

Prelude

A desert, more or less, with a scrubby bush in the foreground, maybe even the dark mouth of a cave. A dying man, fatally wounded by a rifle shot from one of the sheriff's posse that has been pursuing him, is cradled in the arms of a kneeling figure leaning down towards him: a villain in the arms of the law. The man makes a terrible effort to raise himself on an elbow: he has vital information to impart, a missing clue, beans to spill at what might be a Graham-Greene-like moment of redemption before death claims him. His last utterance will reveal the location of the loot, or the whereabouts of the main man. 'It's…it's…' – but the effort is too much. A rattle in the throat. The eyes start. The head slumps to one side. Too late. The man who had been holding him lowers the limp body to the dust.

The truth withheld by fate, or as a plot device – that image recalled from westerns of the fifties, with its wonderful opportunity for an actor to ham it up, is comic enough, but it also makes me want to clamber up on the rickety platform of ageing, in the hope of gaining some kind of view across seventy-eight years. Yet this book is not as I thought it would be. Setting out to celebrate some of the highlights of a lifetime, I find that the role of the accidental, in more than one sense of the word, has been much more prominent than I had realised – temporary shifts of key, as well as an acknowledgement that 'time and chance happen to all men'. A life in which the contingent plays such a part may come closer to farce more often than its leaseholder would like to admit, but at least the admission may ward off hubris.

Less surprisingly, the origins of many sources of wonder lie in the 1960s, my twenties, a time of life apt for the excitement of discoveries powerful enough to be lifelong and not lose any of their intensity. But there are also some that had their beginnings in childhood, and others which occurred much later on.

I've always been clear about what the book is not. Not an apologia, not a donning of sackcloth and ashes, not a surrender to the wan spirit of nostalgia. Nor is it a familial record. Above all, it is written not with the curmudgeonly growl to which some old people are prone, as their opinions harden into nostrums and their hopes into disappointments – but with delight.

Looking back, the world of the 1950s in which I spent my childhood appears in many ways a time of narrow conformities and broad discrimination, including racism. Homosexuality was still a criminal offence, even between consenting adults in private; the last hanging was to take place only in 1964; and the rightful place of women had barely begun to be recognised. You could say that we have problems enough of our own today, including persistent inequalities of wealth and opportunity, the plight of refugees, racism (still), the rise of a crude new nationalism – and with pandemic disease, climate change and nuclear proliferation, the possibility of the destruction of the planet itself. Yet all through the complex trajectory of the years going on, there are new opportunities as well as risks, causes for celebration as well as apprehension.

Quite apart from the changes in society likely to take place during any lifetime, age offers its own insights, among them moments of truth: for instance, a new appreciation of good fortune, suddenly apprehended and simply expressed in the warmth of the sun, the beauty of a landscape or an act of friendship. This has everything to do with an awareness of time running out. I think of my bedridden godfather, dying of liver cancer at sixty, reaching up to grasp me by the lapels, and saying that he would give anything 'for just two years more'. Echoes of Faustian bargains not available to be struck.

Here, in the context of what a judge might call a full

life term, is a collection of times, places and occasions which, like catchy tunes, have continued to demand headroom. Some objects and scenes live on whatever the contingencies or the opaqueness of the plot. They rise clear of their occasion and are hardly to be recruited by narrative. These, too, have their place in the book: among them, bluebells, sea-horses, night airs. Imprinted beyond erasure, they may tell us something about the territory between relative and absolute truth.

1

Moments of truth

' W hat is truth, said jesting Pilate, and would not stay for an answer.' In Egyptian mythology, there were two goddesses of truth to assess the virtue or viciousness of the dead – in effect, one of truth and one of judgement, with the heart of the deceased weighed against the feather of truth. It's a measure that appears inherently flawed: but I hope it could allow that most lives have their good moments of truth, as well as others ineluctably bleak or traumatising. Good moments – which can induce a light head (vertigo, from the Latin *vertex*: summit, zenith, peak) and a light heart, an instant when delight tugs at our mortal tether. Ivan the Terrible, in Eisenstein's film, is surely experiencing just such a moment when he displays his new-born son to the crowd. But even good moments of truth have their risks: in our age of global information, they may seem to imply a glib unawareness of the plight of others. On the other hand, taking good fortune for granted or not allowing the countervailing balance it offers to misfortune seems no better.

And what might truth mean for a given life? 'Who's Who', Auden's 1934 sonnet, opens with the assertion that 'A shilling life will give you all the facts': that is, all the gen., the externals of the sort that make up a *curriculum vitae*, or its current embarrassingly self-advertising form, the Personal Statement. How often does the inner truth seem legible? In Auden's poem, it inheres in the protagonist's deep love for someone who hardly cares, an insouciant whistler who stays at home and potters in the garden. But then there is also the more optimistic perspective suggested by Auden's contemporary Louis MacNeice, in 'Autumn Journal', with the affirmation that '…while a man has voice / He may recover music.'

At the approach to the slope leading down to the undertaker's parlour, there may also come the temptation not just to recover past melody but to beard the future, with last words that are burnished and bright. Think of Alice B. Toklas at the bedside of Gertrude Stein, able to witness Stein asking: 'What is the answer?' and then, when Toklas remained silent, adding, 'In that case, what is the question?', said to be her last words. Even beyond the undertaker, there are such deathless articulations as, for instance, the inscription on the grave of a Scottish minister's wife near Edinburgh: SHE HATH DONE HER BEST. You need to hear the accent in your head, to get the force of what is possibly a tight-lipped sub-text. And there is always Spike Milligan's gag, incised on his headstone: I TOLD YOU I WAS ILL.

When it comes to looking back, many would assent to Hamlet's rhetorical retort to Polonius (in Act II, scene ii) – 'Use every man after his desert and who shall scape whipping?' – and especially so if age brings with it a bite-back of remorse, that wallow-hole of the old. Sometimes properly penitential, it can sag into self-indulgence, a remorseless commination in which most of the verbs are in the conditional perfect. The facts remain unaltered. Past failures cannot be wished away: yet without atonement or expiation, which are not always available, penitence remains abject. In any case, the passage of time is likely to take us to a point well captured by the contemporary poet Lachlan Mackinnon in his poem 'Nocturne':

> At our age, when we have to start to answer
> To ourselves for what we have made of life...

Perhaps the whole notion of trying to recover something of the music is in itself an attempt to find a counterweight to the gravitational pull of the grave, so that in our own judgement the heart can at times really be feather-light.

*

Heartsong

O who could have foretold
That the heart grows old?

W.B. YEATS, 'A Song'

The locked diary of the heart
stores the complete record
in its brisk two-step –
the times when fear or love
made it miss a beat,
sink or leap.

Although it never accuses,
it logs your case exactly,
its archive holds
each crazy wish, each excess,
every instance that has caused it
to soften or harden.

And one day, when perhaps the doctors
come to interpret its scars,
its peaks and troughs,
you, reading over their shoulders,
will see that the heart has remained
as innocent as the Earth itself.

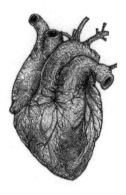

2

Not drowning but waving

A curvetting, at dangerous speed. Sea and wind push the port side down. A seethe of foaming water races the length of the hull, begins to pour over the gunwale. Buries it. The boat starts to go over, is stayed momentarily as if by surface tension. Reaches its tipping-point, is not going to right itself. Less a matter of clutching panic than the simple realisation of what is inescapable. The giddying shock of it.

A great clamour. Flogging sheets, the sails flapping and crackling madly, the boom swinging and bucking. The sails soon wind-wrestled onto the water. More sea rushing in.

This was surely a bad moment of truth. Hardly a revelation to be brooded on at the time, under the circumstances. But it came to me later that I had experienced such a vertiginous sense of revelation only once before, though much less dramatically. When my parents' marriage foundered, my mother left the small farm they had west of Exeter and, taking me and my twin sister Catriona with her (we must have been three or four), sought help from a friend called Buster Baker, who lived in Southborough. I have no picture of her in my head, though 'Buster' suggests the world of Wodehouse. Neither can I remember what her house looked like, or whether she had a family. But still uncomfortably spotlit is the wall of an outbuilding or conservatory at the back of the house, with a sloping roof. On the wall hung a rectangular hoopla board with hooks at which you threw orange rubber quoits rather like the seals on Kilner jars. Playing on my own one day, I somehow managed to land one or possibly two of the quoits on the roof, higher than the guttering and completely out of reach. I knew at once that I would not be able to tell anyone what had happened. Trivial though the incident was, in my mind it must somehow have stood for the complete disruption of our family life at that point, though this was not something I knew at all consciously. I was left with a deep foreboding and a feeling of intense guilt, even shame.

*

The two of us had launched the Albacore, a sleek fifteen-foot sailing dinghy in hot-moulded ply designed by Uffa Fox, from the beach at Dover. Richard McLaughlin, a friend in the same school boarding house as I was, had kindly agreed to come along as crew: we were both seventeen, and between us had a fair bit of sailing experience.

The ostensible reason for the voyage was that I had decided to enter for a Trevelyan Scholarship. Inspired by Kurt Hahn and financed by twelve British companies including United Steel, Guest Keen & Nettlefolds, P. & O., Rolls Royce and Courtaulds, and named in honour of the distinguished historian G.M. Trevelyan, these awards were conceived as a corrective to the perceived narrowness of a purely academic education, as embodied in the then current O and A Level syllabuses.

With the ending of National Service, it was also thought there was a need for some kind of not dissimilar challenge. The Scholarships set out to reward individual initiative, and to this end candidates were to be assessed not only on their school record but also, crucially, on the strength of a project of their own choosing which was to be distinct from the candidate's field of academic study. And the reward was considerable: £500 a year for three years, enough to pay most if not all university bills. The aim was to award up to 34 Scholarships a year, half tenable at Cambridge and half at Oxford: in fact 19 were awarded in the first year, and thereafter between 23 and 27. They did not, however, automatically bring with them a place at either university, so were subject to recipients gaining admission for themselves.

It was also the hope of those who set up the Trevelyan Scholarships that they would attract entries from a range of schools and backgrounds and so play their part, however modestly, in encouraging greater diversification in university applications. The list of Trevelyan Scholars' schools, together with the relatively short duration of the scheme (which ran for eight years), suggest that this aspect was only a qualified success. Ronald Peddie, secretary to the Trust set up to administer the Scholarships, noted (in his 1975 book about the awards) that at least they encouraged some school pupils to apply to Oxbridge who would otherwise never have thought of doing so.

In any case, the imaginative notion of the projects certainly had appeal. Every kind of enquiry and exploration was undertaken, from 'An illustrated and annotated survey of the arms borne by members of the Clopton and Barnardiston families as they occur in some Suffolk churches', to 'Keyhole Covers on Swedish Padlocks', to assorted journeys including canoeing down the Rhine, a four-week stay on the uninhabited Shiant Isles in the Outer Hebrides, and hitch-hiking to Greece to study the island of Hydra and its role in the Greek War of Independence. Rumour had it that one promising application, a study of the breeding habits of ants in mid-France, could not be assessed since the only known expert had expired. Be that as it may, nerds and swots were evidently not to be excluded altogether.

I only found out about the Scholarships from the congratulations offered in school assembly to a pupil who had won one, a boy called Stanley Johnson, whose later projects were to include Boris. The official record describes his entry as 'The Teddy Boy Problem as observed in West Ham.'

*

It seemed to me that the plan I had in mind would be enjoyable and exciting, whether or not there turned out to be a Trevelyan Scholarship at the end of it. It relied – too heavily, as it turned out, on information gleaned from a book on French inland waterways, and envisaged that once across the Channel we would head south along the canal system, progressing by hitching lifts from barges heading down to the Rhône. In a rather obvious attempt to invest the undertaking with some sense of intellectual respectability, we were to take a portable tape recorder and register conversations with people we encountered. There was even talk of noting the differences in regional accents. In retrospect the whole thing, however naïve, seems to have generated sufficient energy and self-belief to see it through, whatever its haziness. But it would certainly have been found wanting by today's health and safety standards. We did tell the Dover coastguards what we were planning, and agreed to ring them from Calais before midnight to report our safe arrival, as indeed we did. As for finding our way, we had an R.A.F. grid compass, Admiralty charts and a roller rule. These instruments, along with a local tide table, would enable us to calculate the likely tidal offset and currents sufficiently well, we thought, for us not to have to use the hand flares which we also took with us.

Initially it seemed that everything was destined to succeed. We set off on a bright, breezy morning and made the crossing in five hours and one minute, thanks to an exhilarating steady wind of Force 4 to 5. We hadn't given any thought to where we might go on arrival in Calais – 'On n'est pas sérieux quand on a dix-sept ans', as Rimbaud began his poem 'Roman'. As it was, we were lucky – and grateful – to be welcomed by members of the local yacht club, who had seen us coming in to the harbour and generously let us sleep in the clubhouse. When it transpired that the barges we were planning to hitch lifts with were not going south at that time of year, heading north to Belgium and the Dutch islands, sailing when we could and getting tows when we couldn't, was a Plan B easily dreamt up on the spot. And even when we made the mistake of leaving our mast at Calais, so that we could pass under low bridges across the canals we had decided to include on a circuitous route back to the coast, our luck held. When we had gone back to Calais and retrieved it, and were trudging along the road with the thing on our shoulders, two very obliging Mancunians in a small grey Austin van (WOM 112) stopped for us and gamely tied the mast onto their roof-rack.

All continued to go well as we headed up the Belgian coast. We touched briefly on a sandbank off Nieuwpoort, but got free easily enough by lifting the centreboard and gybing: and when, later, we ran into a bank of sea fog, from whose interior a mournful horn lowed at us, that didn't prevent a good run to Ostend. From there, we went on to the almost-island of Walcheren – first to Flushing, then northwards up the canal to Zieriksee, and to Veere. We did manage to get a tow from a motor-sailer part of the way: for the rest, we had to paddle the boat ourselves, or pull it by its painter, taking turns along the towpath. And then? Aiming to reach the Friesian Islands, we were aware that our progress so far was slow. We set off from Veere heavily reefed down, following an uncertain forecast of wind force 4 gusting to force 8. Before we left I unpacked our emergency flares and put them within reach – just in case, or as an act of superstitious optimism, like someone wearing a heavy coat in the hope that this would make rain unlikely.

Once we were out of the lee of the land, and not far below the Hook of Holland, things got worse, with a hefty sea running and the boat yawing quite badly. And then, luffing up in an attempt to gain greater control, we met too large a wave on our starboard quarter. It can't have helped that we had removed one of the buoyancy bags in the bow compartment, to allow more storage space: and the small coaming on either side of the mast, more decorative than practical, certainly wasn't going to keep the North Sea out. And didn't.

We righted the boat by standing on the centreboard, but it was no good: we had shipped too much water, and any attempt to make way ended with slewing to a halt after only a few yards. We let off five of our six red flares. A wave knocked the striker of the sixth out of my hand: the next wave brought it back. At some point Richard became separated from the boat. I threw him a line, but it fell short. Thank God we had our lifejackets. He was sighted further south towards the mouth of the Maas, by a boat that might have seen our flares as it passed in the distance. Two hours or so later, a Dutch coastguard cutter appeared, with Richard on board. Our rescuers did their best to get the Albacore in tow, but it was difficult, and the dinghy's hull was holed by a boathook. In the end it proved necessary to run the cutter onto a sandbank: skilfully done, and the damage to the dinghy was countered by the coastguards' generosity in not seeking to claim salvage, to which they were likely to have been entitled.

It proved impossible to find a Dutch boatyard prepared to undertake repairs to the hull: in the end the Albacore had to be shipped back to England (for all our naïvety we had taken out insurance, though it was surprising enough that any underwriter had accepted the risk). In London, I had to report to an office in the City dealing with salvaged and shipwrecked yachts. I have a memory of an official perched on a high stool quizzing me about the gross tonnage of the vessel and the number of berths.

When I wrote it all up for the Trevelyan assessors, my account ended with the North Sea débâcle. Two interviews followed, one in London and the final one in Cambridge, both beginning with the question 'And then…?' As it was, I then got one of the awards.

3

Give and take

As the 1611 Authorised Version of the bible has it, when Paul spoke at Miletus to elders of the congregation from Ephesus, he quoted the words of Jesus: 'It is more blessed to give than to receive.' Three hundred and fifty years on, the New English Bible (1961) renders this as 'Happiness lies more in giving than in receiving.' The emendation of approval from a higher authority to a recipe for personal satisfaction is an interesting one: an instance of what gets glossed in translation, perhaps, or a clue to changing times. Either way, it's an adage for adults only, to which no child would assent at Christmas since the night when St Nicholas, in a moment of generosity, tossed three bags of gold down the chimney of an impoverished family. They landed, with an exactness which would have been fluky had it not clearly been providential, in socks hung above the fireplace to dry. Since then it has at Christmas been distinctly more blessed to receive than to give.

*

You woke early in the winter dark: sometimes too early, out of excitement, only to find that nothing had changed. But then it did: waking again, you were aware of a considerable weight towards the end of the bed, which you could probe gently with your foot. A squeaky weight. A lumpy weight. On with the bedside light. The stocking which you had left lying across the bedcover the night before, flat and empty, was now bulbous, crammed with things that stuck out at all angles.

You set to. Some items were given a cursory glance, others a closer inspection. Soon there would be a scatter of loot across the bed – crayons (more crayons!), a balloon, notebooks (another notebook!), a wooden or steel puzzle, a tiny snow-globe, a small cylinder of liquid soap for blowing bubbles, sweets, chocolate, a small wooden top, assorted gewgaws... In some years there would be an item in a class of its own, such as a gyroscope which could balance on a miniature Eiffel Tower as it span. And every year you knew you had come to the end when you reached the tangerine wrapped in tissue paper in the toe of the stocking. It was all thrilling, even if the pile of presents, once scooped together alongside the litter of screwed-up paper and packaging, looked surprisingly insignificant in comparison to the crammed lumpiness you started out with: but then stocking gifts had to be modest if they were to fit.

Before self-consciousness sets in, or the insidious promptings of advertising and retail competitiveness, children not only receive gifts with complete naturalness, but bestow them in the same way too. This can involve a rigorous test of parental diplomacy, as in the case of the bouquet composed of viper's bugloss, red valerian, primroses and ragged robin my sister and I once collected from the hedgerow and presented as an already wilting bunch to our mother. Her show of gratitude convinced us completely. She managed an even more impressive encore when, having only nine pence to spend and on the advice of a local shopkeeper, we bought her a bottle of pink cleaner for glass, Windolene. It cannot have been more than the thought that counted.

In later childhood, perhaps only the excitement of a first bike could match the stocking gifts. By then, it was also a matter of thank-you letters: a real drag, and knowing they were appropriate and had to be done didn't make them any easier, rather the reverse. They seemed disproportionately burdensome even when you felt real gratitude for the gift in question.

Later still, modesty can re-assert itself. When the gift comes from a lover, the least object – say, a small bowl, a vase, a holder smelling sweetly of pine needles, even its ribbon and wrapping – is taken as evidence of love's truth, acquiring a totemic value well in excess of its cost. The same goes for some family gifts, too, especially those handed down from generation to generation, their worth often magnified by the absence of the original owner. For me, this also meant three of my father's paintings, given to me on separate occasions in the course of his rare visits. There is a watercolour of two tall ships under full sail on a calm sea; an oil painting of the Adriatic island of Korčula; and a cleverly conceived gouache showing the fish market at Barcelona almost as a theatre stage with, in the foreground, a boat, a lantern and fish seen within a surround of draped nets; behind them, the sea and the outline of a huddle of buildings are darkly visible.

One of the most attractive forms of giving was the spontaneity sometimes shown by my cousin Pam. If you expressed admiration for something in her house – for example, one of her pretty, small shallow dishes with flowers painted on enamel over copper, she was quite likely to suggest that you keep it. It wasn't easy to accept a gift proffered in this way, I suppose for fear of appearing covetous and because I knew that she herself liked the object in question, having chosen it. Maybe in our culture we are too easily embarrassed by such open generosity.

Inherited gifts are by definition a matter of receiving. (Happily, few are as sly as Villon's bequest to his old foe Thibault d'Aussigny, the Bishop of Orléans. Only six verses in to 'Le Testament' he bestows on him 'Le verselet script septiesme / Du pséaulme *Deus Laudem'* – verse 7 of Psalm 109, 'Let his days be few: and let another take his office'. Not to mention the gift of that poisoned apple offered to Snow White, or the present the Greeks left for the Trojans – 'Timeo Danaos et dona ferentes', as Virgil rhythmically warns in the *Aeneid*.

The one gift I cherish above all others came to me from my mother, to whom it was given by her father as a twenty-first birthday present. A baby grand piano made in 1911, the year of my mother's birth, in most domestic settings it looks big enough to belie its name. All through my life it has dominated whichever room houses it: and it would always be the climax of any house-moving operation. After its lid, keyboard cover and music stand had been detached, the pedals removed and all three sets of legs unscrewed, it was tipped on its side, bedded in felt, secured with canvas straps and heaved onto the low platform of a trolley with wheels. Two men at least were required to lift and shift it. In one house it had to be manoeuvred up a flight of stairs, summoning the memory of a piano cascading out of control in the opposite direction, down a flight of steps, in the Laurel and Hardy film *The Music Box*.

Like all baby grands, the shape of it is somewhat tubby, sturdy rather than elegant, though something of that too when the lid is lifted and propped on its stick. On the inside of the keyboard cover, visible only when it is raised, and inlaid in a wood lighter than the rosewood of the casing are the words:

JOHN BROADWOOD & SONS

LONDON

London! Where I had been born and which, as a child living in Exeter, I firmly believed to be the centre of the universe, a glittering hub from which I had for the moment been exiled, and to which I would surely return. Not that the piano depended on this association for its magic. It was a system complete in itself, with its hammers, dampers and pins, its gold pedals shaped like shoe inners, the bass and treble strings racing to cross at an angle to one another; and then, the wing of the lid, the broad tabs of the fifty-five white keys and the narrower, raised black keys arranged in alternating groups of two and three. It was not only a musical instrument but a sustaining pedal for the imagination, able to project the slightest or wildest improvisation as the harbinger of a glittering future career as performer or even composer. It had other roles too: as a refuge, a shadowy canopy under which you could hide well out of adult sight. And if a tsunami should suddenly engulf the house, surely it would float away intact, with the family crouched in the soundbox, a painter attached to the hole in the iron frame and the lid prop available as a boathook. In the event of a bombing raid, we would be able to shelter under its wing, safe beneath the protection of our household god.

The passage of time has given it an added patina of near-permanence. The piano has always been there: and still is, even in the age of the electronic keyboard and amid the plethora of sound sources. And to hear it played now with considerable skill by my daughters, knowing that it will be handed on to them, is a gift in its own right.

4

Bluebells

From multiples, they merge to a single infusing colour; beyond fifteen yards or so the focus is lost. Almost is their colour. Almost lavender, almost mauve, and they escape under cover of such approximations.

A wash, a tide. You could drown, here beneath the bursting beech-buds, in the almost blue slack water of the spring tide. Still as sworn statements, not a stem amongst them moving. Birdsong quiescent, attendant. How can flowers create such a hush?

To the trees' hundreds they bring their thousands, held as one washed soul. Close to, they invite the eye, only to baffle it in their mauve middle distance. Hyacinthoides non-scripta: what could you say you have seen?

You have come to assay what is wordless, priceless. Imagine them gone, with no memorial but birdsong. Is this what ineffable means, inexpressible or unutterable? Slants of sunlight gleam on the slender green leaves. The green without which the almost blue of the bell-flowers would be quite different. Is this also what die blaue Blume *infers, the mystical flower, not a rose, that can never be found and plucked?*

How can such a crowd be so still? Even when a light breeze gets up, the dominant impression remains one of immobility. They stand to attention in the sunlight. Almost deep lilac, not quite mauve, close to a milky mid-purple. None of the above, exactly.

After a time, after a distance, the eye takes them as read. They tip over the wood's inner horizons. More than the sum of themselves, they state all that can be, in full flower. They have nothing to prove: if they trap the mind, it is on their own terms. Not invulnerable, but always singing. Their tender salad is stronger than the grey and green trunks of the beech-trees that stand everywhere amongst them and rise far above. It would be good to think them invincible. It would be good to think they are safe, in the acres of papery mast.

Start again.

Though they are motionless, the wind moves among them, like a miracle-worker biding his time. Consider the soft droop of the bells hung from the fragile overhead stems, each with its curled-back frill at the flower's mouth.

Jacinthe des bois, Glockenblume: *the shush of the French, the glottal sounding of the German.*

The pale filaments. Intensities of the shade: however broad and sunlit the wood, the bluebells ward their secret, their infection of colour.

Two gunshots. Later, three more, away at the edge of the

wood's hollow lumber-room acoustic.

The scrupulous silence re-establishes itself.

The bluebells are uniform in height and stance, so that the eye cannot get past them. They are non-transferable, and easily evade being held properly in photos or paintings. Non-scripta, non-picta. Like grief and joy, they soon show words and pigments their limits.

They sing without words. Lydian purple and azure put together, almost.

All their best associations are multiples of themselves: isolated in a vase, they are hopelessly lessened. Even in small clumps in city gardens, diminished. In the wood, nothing denies them: they sing in unison, time their only counterpoint.

The colour becomes a voice, a mode. The haze of them, a humming haze.

You could think they are advancing, that soon you will be calf-deep in them, wading through. But they surge in the mind only, under the fluted pillars of the trees.

Start again.

Perhaps you have been looking too long among the bluebells: they are beginning to chill you. Their colour grows more intense by the minute...closer at hand than before, the pout of another gunshot.

It would not be possible to withstand such intensity for long. Sooner rather than later, the blue tide surging to crash over your head. Even from one look to the next the colour fluctuates, as the glister of sunlight picks out one or another diagonal strip.

Imagine rolling up the whole floor of them! Or at least being able to warehouse them in your memory. Impossible – here experience is meaning: even beauty, perhaps, truth. Their scent, sweet close to, doesn't seem to spread its waft.

It is a colour not unlike one taken from the sheen of spilt petrol: but a wash, a seethe, lacking the texture of surface.

If this were a dream, there would be no other possible dream beyond it.

The bluebells forgive the trees their jaggedness, their whitened fallen limbs, their untidiness. In their own community, they know nothing of solos.

As if finely shaken down from overhead, as a pigment that covers everything: as if able to invoke stillness just by being, an untrodden apartness that absorbs nothing while affecting everything…But I hear unreal voices in a far room, the indoor echo of them along one of the woodland tracks.
Start again.

Not to be fashioned, or arranged in any artistic version or vision of spring. Look again – a mixing of indigo and mid-blue, almost. A broadcasting of the random.

A Mendelian aberration, almost. I've only ever seen two people with bluebell-coloured eyes: like the flowers, they made the eyes of anyone looking at them brim and swim.

They gain on you, these flowers. And only now I notice that the notebook I'm writing in has a woven cover of blue and green material.

The open secret of the bluebell wood. Have you ever seen, even in those Venetian shops selling a great number and variety of powdered pigments, a single one which could be described as being the exact *colour of the bluebell?*

*

Later, at night, when I close my eyes, I find an after-image intact: and the precise bluebell-blue, above the green bedding.

5

'Behold, the sea itself'

from Sea Pictures

The sea laps to shore like a well-trained pet,
the water clear enough to cast shadows
on its smooth ground. Or snaps a mast,
shouts at you, has the sails flogging
like pumped-up ghosts. Never look to the sea
for consistency.

*

On a summer night, when the salt breeze
blows steady and warm, it sometimes happens

as it twists low past riding hulls,
with the land shrunk into darkness, that the sea
will relax and throw the whole sky
wide open.

*

I can't remember a time when I didn't love the sea. It has always been a given, but never taken for granted. It certainly hasn't been a matter of immersion. Like many of my generation, I learned to swim quite late in childhood and, however much I might have longed to do the crawl, I have never been much more than a breaststroke wallower, more liable to sink than swim and hardly more buoyant than a lead weight. For me the calm of the chlorinated pool was quite testing enough, and the salt gag of the corrugated sea an alarming complication.

In retrospect I can sight an assortment of seamarks, in literature as in life, from the owl and the pussycat lucky enough to sail away for all that time, to the exultant cry of Xenophon's men when at last they reached the coast; from the sea running out across the sands at Exmouth, to the way it rattled the pebbles on the beach at Budleigh Salterton. The sea was well represented in school assemblies, too – the stirring intercession for 'they that go down to the sea in ships, and occupy their business in great waters'; that 'eternal father strong to save / Whose arm doth bind the restless wave'. And then, in English lessons, Tennyson's crossing of the bar, Masefield's dirty British coaster.

What of people who, like me, cannot recall their first sighting of the sea? There must be others who have never actually seen it, except in pictures or stories. Can their imagination accommodate the curve of the homeless horizon, or see the foaming wavelets break at the edge of some palm-fringed lagoon? Is their sea slate grey, aquamarine or turquoise?

What's clear is the impossibility of fixing the sea in a single image. Whatever the medium – words, paint, film – something of it remains tantalisingly out of reach. It has the politician's gift for contradiction, for assuming any number of Protean guises. It is, among other things, a sky-mirror, a mirror of the soul, rubbish tip, keeper of secrets, harbourer of strange and beautiful plants and life-forms, battlefield, graveyard, agency of love or death, white sails or black sails, imposer of exile and enabler of a return to the home port. In the twenty-first century, it bears witness to urgent environmental threats and needs. Beyond artistry and metaphor, the glaciers are shrinking, the coral dying, the minute particulates of profligacy insinuating themselves everywhere.

*

I can no more imagine the sea's absence from my writing than I could the impact such an erasure would have on those Devon and Somerset coastal lanes that rise steeply to the reaches of high air. Led forward by high hedges on either side, the eye focuses naturally on the bright openness of the sky ahead: somehow that blankness of pearly grey or clear blue conveys the presence of the salt acres below. Even without a map or local knowledge, you would intuit your closeness to the land's edge. There is something in this early perception of the sea's proximity which cannot entirely be explained in terms of the clues that come later, as you get closer – onshore breezes, the smack of salt on your lips, the tangy whiff of the tides.

*

From my childhood in Exeter, I keep two vivid early memories of the sea. In one, on a day trip to Fowey, I am standing on a slipway close to the harbour wall, looking out at moored boats. There are stone steps going down the side of the wall to a small landing stage where the green clear water laps invitingly, with small boats pirouetting and tugging at their painters in the pull of the tide. I knew then that gazing at the sea would not be enough: I had to be on it. Which leads to the second memory, of occasional excursions to Exmouth, which in good weather might include the

'Trip round the Bay' advertised on a blackboard at the top of the beach. You got onto the boat, a large open one with a satisfying chugger of an engine and a good wobbliness, by going up a springy plank bridging the shallows between beach and boat. With any luck the sea would then provide its own springiness and by the time the boat rounded the melancholy clanging bell-buoy off Orcombe Point to head back, there could be a real swell running.

*

I was released, so to speak, in the same year as the film *In which we serve*, co-directed by David Lean and Noël Coward, and my childhood coincided with any number of films about the Second World War in which the sea played a central part. They almost all seemed to feature one or other permutation of Jack Hawkins, John Mills, Donald Sinden and Richard Attenborough. Festooned with outsize binoculars and peering out from their soft halters of white polo-neck sweaters, they scanned the horizon anxiously for enemy cruisers and U-boats, or skulked in their own submarine, periscope down, maintaining radio silence while the enemy passed overhead or prepared to unleash vicious depth charges. Sometimes the Pathé News would report a drama at sea: one of the most memorable was the foundering in the Atlantic, in January 1952, of the American freighter

Flying Enterprise and the subsequent heroism of her skipper, Captain Kurt Carlsen, who insisted on staying on board while the salvage tug *Turmoil* tried to tow her to Falmouth. Such documentary excitement, more often than not geared to suggest another specifically British achievement, was easily matched by films like *The Crimson Pirate*, which also came out in 1952 and had Burt Lancaster swooping tirelessly, sword in hand, from ratlines to gun-deck.

But the approaches to the real sea lay elsewhere, in the room of our dentist, Mr Rainey. This was improbable. In the early fifties there wasn't much to commend a visit to the dentist, where what awaited you was the terrible slow drill with its grinding vibration. 'Watch the rabbit running round!' said Mr Rainey, attaching a scrap of cotton wool to the drill's belt drive and fooling no one: you knew that, half concealed behind his back, he was holding a large syringe that had holes along its sides, like those on a sten gun to allow for the escape of gases – and then there was also the threat, rarely mentioned but known about, of gas itself. In this case, however, there was a redeeming feature. Mr Rainey knew of a sailing club, the Island Cruising Club, recently formed at Salcombe in South Devon. Founded by a Bedalian, John Bayley, the club had as its flagship *Provident*, a Brixham trawler built in 1924, and there was also a slightly smaller and older boat, *Hoshi*, a schooner dating from 1909.

Provident under full sail was impressive: a gaff ketch 95 feet long and weighing 85 tonnes, she had tan sails and a green hull. The sight of her leaving or entering harbour at the beginning or end of a cruise was unforgettable. But it was dinghy sailing that appealed to me more, with its greater immediacy and closeness to the water, wind and weather: a closeness that kept you finely suspended between excitement and the edge of fear. Luckily, the club did offer courses in dinghy sailing, with participants accommodated in an old Motor Torpedo Boat anchored round the corner from Salcombe, in the lower part of the Kingsbridge estuary known as the Bag. I went on several week-long courses, starting with learning the basics in the club's traditional gaff-rigged dinghies, clinker-built 14-footers. Later on, there was the chance to sail a National 12 or one of the club's two Swordfish dinghies (15 feet and carvel, in plywood), as well as a dark blue Enterprise with fetching lighter blue sails (a new boat then, designed by Jack Holt and the first boat to be sponsored by a newspaper, *The News Chronicle*.) It was one of the great virtues of the club that it didn't lay particular emphasis on racing, which featured simply as an occasional test of competence undertaken for fun. I can understand the excitement of it, but I've always thought that there is more than enough competitiveness on land: the sea is worth more than that.

The sheer beauty of Salcombe played its part. When you first saw the sea, as you approached the town, you looked from the heights of the cliffs, or from the hill above North Sands, onto all the glory of its shifting colours. Sometimes a steely grey, it was more often a brilliant aquamarine, or turquoise, or green.

Sooner or later I acquired the accoutrements of obsession: *Reed's Nautical Almanac*, the Island Cruising Club's pennant and, best of all, a large serrated sailor's knife and a marlin spike, the two of them together in a bulky leather sheath. I still have them.

I became so enamoured of it all that I agreed readily when the club asked whether I would be a guinea-pig for the Duke of Edinburgh's Awards scheme, which was thinking of setting up a marine component (I did not know that Kurt Hahn – like my father, a refugee from Germany, had a hand in developing the scheme, as he would later in setting up the Trevelyan Scholarships). I was to spend twenty-four hours in the estuary in one of the club's dinghies, with one other as crew. We were to fend for ourselves, and would be allowed to beach the boat overnight and sleep on the foreshore. This was duly done without trouble, and a report sent off to Sir John Hunt, then Director of the Awards. Later, a second expedition was mounted – this time in a very heavy boat of 20 feet or so brought round from Mevagissey to Plymouth, where we collected it. It was a cumbersome old thing, better at making leeway than sailing at all close to the wind, and with running backstays that had to be let off or tightened whenever the boat manoeuvred. This time there were three of us, and the plan was to venture out of the estuary and round the coast. As before, we would be allowed to land, and we towed a shallow saucer of a pram dinghy to take us ashore, since the weight and draft of the boat made it likely that we would have to anchor offshore. We even had a primus stove.

Off we went, past the Wolf Rock, over the bar, out to Start Point, where we turned north-east to head up the coast in the direction of Dartmouth. At some point, while we were anchored in a bay, a saucepanful of hot water was spilt from the primus onto my right foot, scalding it. I had to go ashore in the pram, which was caught by an inroading wave and capsized as it was nearing the shore: the scalded foot got a cauterizing dose of salt. Holidaymakers on the beach dosed me less painfully with aspirin and the brandy they said they always had with them, and either they or some other Samaritan drove me to a doctor. End of expedition.

(This incident was a near-repetition of an experience much earlier in my childhood when, sitting on the lap of a Land Army girl who was helping my parents on the farm, I managed to pull down a large kettle filled with hot water onto myself. I still remember how the woollen dressing-gown I was wearing clung to me like the shirt of Nessus. At least this later mishap did not require hospitalisation and skin grafts.)

Another report went off to Sir John Hunt, and I heard nothing more.

*

On three occasions I've travelled, at the opposite end of the spectrum to dinghy sailing, on large steamers – one British, one Greek, and one Italian. At some point towards the end of my time at university I responded to a small newspaper announcement I had spotted, which sought a crew to sail a catamaran from Hong Kong to England. Irresistible, especially as like most of my contemporaries I had no clear idea of what I wanted to do when I fell off the top of the educational ladder. After meeting the owner in London I was taken on, as was a young woman called Belinda, who had far greater experience of cruising in sizeable boats than I had.

We set off from Southampton on the *Chusan*, a P. & O. ship of more than 24,000 tons and about the length of two football fields. The voyage lasted almost three weeks and took in Suez, Aden, Mumbai, Colombo, Singapore and Penang on the way. Day after day of looking down from the high deck at the bucking stern as it lifted, slewed and settled back into the next trough; and of wondering at the great grey-green marbling of the ocean surface, the seethe and hiss of foam as the ship drove effortfully forward. Often, nothing else to be seen as far as the horizon, other than the swooping and soaring escort of gulls across the wake. Below deck, wonderful meals and, for those of us travelling in the cheapest berths, salt water baths.

The accident happened before we even got there: while Belinda and I were on our way out the catamaran, while on its mooring, was hit by a typhoon. We reached Hong Kong to find that the boat was being repaired, but slowly: when we went to see it, it took an effort to imagine it fully restored. Sadly, the project fizzled out. Belinda went home, and I found myself beached in lodgings in the Chungking Mansions, Kowloon, with ever dwindling resources. I explored various options, including the possibility of teaching for a time in a World Lutheran Federation school or at the Diocesan High School: but these possibilities would be available only some months after I would have run out of money altogether. In the end, I managed to get a cheap ticket on a Greek boat going back to Piraeus, the *Patris*. Once the *Bloemfontein Castle* but renamed and now owned by the Chandris line, it plied between Australia and Greece. The journey was memorable chiefly for the storm we encountered in the Strait of Malacca: a real bone-and-hull rattler, enough to increase considerably the already considerable intake of Foster's among the Australian passengers (the ship had begun its journey in Sydney), while many of the Greeks who made up the complement of travellers packed their bags and, kneeling beside their belongings in the passageways, resorted to prayer.

A not dissimilar incident was to colour a journey back from Kenya at the end of a teaching contract, aboard the MV *Victoria*, a Lloyd Triestino ship headed for Barcelona. Running into a fierce storm between Mombasa and Cape Town, the ship's captain decided not to reduce speed, as the schedule had already been disrupted by a strike of the crew before departure from Karachi. The result was dramatic: the forward masthead light was knocked out, furniture in the largely deserted public rooms careered wildly like fairground waltzers, and there was considerable damage to a number of the cars being transported in the open on the foredeck.

For me, such excitements only added to the power of the sea's embrace.

*

'Behold, the sea itself' – I love the rhetorical flourish of that line of Whitman's, aptly presented in an exhilaration of brass and voices at the opening of Vaughan Williams's *A Sea Symphony*. The almost tautological 'sea itself' seems halfway to an acknowledgement of the impossibility of trapping such a quicksilver element. You might well think, though, that of all the arts music would be the one best able to catch something of the sea's endless changes of tempo, rhythm and mood, the interplay of light and shadow, undertow and overfalls, dark and dazzle. And has any composer achieved this more effectively than Debussy? *La Mer*, which the composer described as 'three symphonic sketches', has indicative titles and notes for each of its components:

1. 'From dawn to noon on the sea' – very slow – becoming gradually more animated ['De l'aube à midi sur la mer' – très lent – animez peu à peu].

2. 'Play of the waves' – allegro (with a very versatile rhythm) – animated ['Jeux des vagues' – allegro (dans un rhythme très souple) – animé].

3. 'Dialogue of the wind and the sea' – animated and tumultuous – ease up very slightly ['Dialogue du vent et de la mer' – animé et tumultueux – cédez très légèrement].

Sparse directions, but enough to give some idea of Debussy's intentions. In fact the music captures brilliantly the sea's sinuous power, its muscular flexibility, its reinventions. The French composer Jean Barraqué describes *La Mer* as 'un devenir sonore', while Caroline Potter, in *The Cambridge Companion to Debussy*, writes of his use of 'a multitude of water figurations that could be classified as musical onomatopoeia: they evoke the sensation of swaying movement of waves and suggest the pitter-patter of falling droplets of spray'. But this is not programme music: one of its chief characteristics is a taking up and exploration of successive possibilities for which 'sketches' seems exactly the right description.

My vinyl LP of *La Mer* has as its cover Monet's 1886 painting depicting a point on the Brittany coast at Belle-Ile: dark cliffs and a sea of blue, violet and green, with a tumult of white waves dashed onto the rocks. For painters, capturing the nature of the sea must be a particular challenge – how can such a continual coming and going, such shifting weather, such vastness be caught in a static frame? Even such realistic representations as Dutch seascapes of the 17th century, with their dramatic scenes of rearing waves that threaten ships broached to or close to foundering under skies engrossed with billowing storm clouds – even these are a convention, a stylisation. As is the product of a very different culture, Hokusai's *The Great Wave off Kanagawa*, a gigantic rearing pillar of water curled over at the top, about to topple and break. If you look carefully you can make out the little boats it is about to engulf, so diminutive that they hardly seem worthy of its attention. It was a detail from this painting which was reproduced on the cover of the first edition of the score of *La Mer*, published by A. Durand & Fils in 1905.

When I think of the sea as it features in some of my father's paintings, it is never roused or angry but essentially decorative, there for its colour, a simple context for boats in harbour or drawn up on a shore: static, not a primary focus, at best a sheen of light.

Amongst contemporary artists who make the sea their subject (and how many of them are there?), I greatly admire the work of Norman Ackroyd. His etchings of Scottish and Irish islands and the seas surrounding them have an astonishing capacity to render almost kinetically the movement and mood of the waters. Seen sometimes in clear light, but often in a haze of spume and poor visibility, these rock massifs from which spray and scatters of wheeling birds fly up convey a powerful atmospheric, a context in which the surging cross-seas swell, regroup, are funnelled into distance. The etching process, with such discipline inherent in the production of different states, certainly demands fine judgement on the part of the artist: and I wonder whether the results, with their subtle monochrome exploitation of tone and nuance, aren't in their way more liberating for the viewer's empathetic imagination than colour might be, enhancing but never exaggerating the dramatic qualities of the pictures. And

Ackroyd has returned again and again to such subjects: a memorable image in a 2013 BBC documentary (in the series 'What do Artists Do All Day?') shows him looking at a map of Britain's northern islands, and musing that there is 'enough stuff here for a dozen lifetimes'. It is in the integrity of these revisitations, which match so well the sea's endless new versions of itself, that the staying power of his work resides.

*

In reality, the sea often expresses itself as much in the ear as the eye. In the rich trickle of water under the hull, quickening from gurgle to rising surge as the wind drives the boat forward into the flow; by proxy, in the sounds of the wind itself, its steady beat or its fluctuations. The element becomes inseparable from its effects – the tensing of the rigging: a sudden tautness as the boat gathers way, as if called to attention. Then, alerting all the senses, a frisky lightness like that of a live animal, in response to the least adjustment of the tiller, or the slackening or tightening of sheets: the quick heeling over when close-hauled, the exhilarating sitting up of the hull on a reach. Planing, the boat is supreme, riding masterfully on the sea's back. And, by way of contrast, the looseness of running before the wind, something close to a giddy rolling, like a drunkard just about in control of himself...something approaching Rimbaud's drunken boat. In 'Le Bateau Ivre' the poet's sensibility has become the vessel itself, an intoxication at the mercy of the element and actually almost indistinguishable from it:

Et dès lors, je me suis baigné dans le Poème
De la Mer, infusé d'astres, et lactescent,
Dévorant les azurs verts; où, flottaison blême
Et ravi, un noyé pensif parfois descend.

(And from that moment on, I bathed in the Poem
Infused with stars, lactating, the Poem of the Sea,
Devourer of green azures; where, ecstatic, wan,
A thoughtful drowned man occasionally drifts down.)

Maybe that is the closest you can get to it. Certainly it is true for me, to put it in Charles Trenet's somewhat salt-cracked voice, that 'La mer / A bercé mon cœur pour la vie.' Swash, backwash, systole, diastole: it's all there.

6

Worth your dreams

B y the time we got to Petra, we were already
almost sated with new sights and experiences.
Among them, the drive down through Austria,
Yugoslavia and Bulgaria, some of it at night and on
tortuous mountain roads, often in the dusty wake of
huge lorries; Istanbul, a pulsating, crowded revelation;
Baalbek, with its massive, half-tumbled pillars that we
had only ever seen on Lebanese stamps; the old part
of Jerusalem, then in Jordan, and including the Via
Dolorosa and the Dome of the Rock.

It was the summer of 1962, and there were three of
us, all at the end of our first year at Oxford – Peter
studying classics, and John, history (for me, it was
French and German). We travelled with youthful
carelessness, in our own version of a road movie that
preferred to steer clear of what was too obvious, in
a spirit of mild defiance that found the momentum
and incidents of journeying every bit as exciting as
whatever sights or sites we might visit along the way.

Being proved wrong in this, though, was part of the pleasure. And for all our woolly thinking, at least we had had the sense to go on an Owners' Maintenance Course at the Rover factory in Solihull, so that on the journey we were able to service our second-hand Land Rover ourselves.

I've always liked the Michelin Guide's gradations of approval in its estimation of places: in ascending order, 'vaut la visite', 'vaut le détour' and, as the ultimate accolade, 'vaut le voyage'. For Petra, it might be necessary to invent an even higher category – 'vaut vos rêves', perhaps. Worth your dreams.

*

We are required to leave the Land Rover at the local police station at Wadi Musa, where we are offered donkeys but decline them, preferring to walk. We set off along the Siq, a track leading between red sandstone cliffs: underfoot, a mixture of earth, grass and pebbles. Hemmed in, narrower in some places, broader in others, after a kilometre the path continues in deep shadow. Then, at the final turn, a slit of astonishing brightness ahead, a jagged vertical dazzle blinding in the morning sunlight. Ahead, coming into view only at the last minute and almost too close to take in, the high pink stone frontage of a building that in its grandeur has the appearance of a temple or palace,

with columns, pediment and, at its apex, what looks
like a large ceremonial urn. Above it all, just below
the narrow gap left for sky, the surface of the cliff face
shows where the carvers cut back into the rock. It is
one of the marvels of Petra that no stone was brought
here from outside: the buildings are hewn from the
solid rock already there.

We have read about Petra before our journey: we
know that it was the stronghold of the Nabataean
arabs, whose power derived from the city's location
on an important spice route, as well as their skill in
agriculture, stone carving and harvesting rainwater.
The city was at its zenith in the first century CE, but
then fell to the Romans, before new sea trade routes
diminished its importance. In 363 an earthquake
destroyed many of the buildings (there were thought
to be some eight hundred by then). Eventually Petra
was abandoned.

But the moment in Petra's history we most relate to,
as we stand there in wonderment, is its rediscovery by
the traveller Johann Burckhardt, who in 1812 simply
walked into the forgotten place. We seem to have done
much the same.

The building facing us, Al Khazna (the Treasury),
is not in fact a temple, though it may once have been
the mausoleum of the Nabataean king Aretas IV. In
front of it a man is sitting on a low stool – a custodian

perhaps, and the only person around. We signal greetings to one another, and gather from his relaxed attitude that we are free to explore. And here comes another astonishment – finding that this grand fanfare of a façade has nothing behind it but a dark space, speluncar, crudely scooped out of the rock. The same turns out to be true of the other buildings: whole cliff frontages of them stretch away, leaning back into the rock from which they have been carved, in varying states of degradation and so eroded by the desert wind that they have acquired a wonderful fluidity, as if seen through water, as *engloutis* as Debussy's cathedral. This gives them a dream-like quality heightened by the upside-down look of cut-out door holes, and by the overall impression of streaky bacon suggested by their patterning, vivid striations of rust-red, grey-blue, white.

In the silence of the gathering heat we spend the day exploring this place so unlike anywhere else we have been. When night falls we sleep stretched out on the ground, in the womb-like darkness behind the frontage of the Treasury. No sign of the man we had met earlier. In the morning, we get up stiffly to see sunlight fire the rosy stone once more.

*

Thirty-eight years on, I visited Petra again – this time

with my wife Helen, and our friends Laurie and Fiona. The battered second-hand Land Rover has transmogrified into our friends' gleaming black Jeep. It was the first of many changes which, taken together, made this second visit in its way as oneiric as the earlier one had been.

If the Wadi Musa police station was still there, it was well camouflaged by the cluster of hotels that had sprung up close to the path leading to Petra, just visible on the far side of a stout perimeter fence, gate and kiosk. We booked in at one of the hotels, and were advised to get up early the next morning if we wanted to be ahead of the crowds. It would cost the equivalent of about £25 each to get in, but the ticket would be valid for two or three days.

We were at the entrance by the time it opened at six in the morning, part of a small crowd. This time we were offered horses rather than donkeys, and declined them. The Siq path had been resurfaced, and the channels for water running at waist height in the rocks alongside looked as if they had been restored. As we got closer to the end of the track, there came the sound of a regular beat, a throbbing that intensified as we walked on. Then, like a moment in a recurring dream, a glimpse of astonishing light, that jagged dazzle...and we found ourselves once again confronting the pink magnificence of the Treasury. But the silence that had informed the 1962 visit with its version of awe had been displaced by the source of the noise we had heard on our way in, the pulsing of generators deployed to power fridges crammed with 7-up, Coca-Cola and orangeade, which stood here and there beside scatters of tables and chairs. There were a few horses too, their heads bedevilled with feverish clusters of flies even this early in the day. A radio tipped music into the air.

Much of the site remained as it had been before: but by the time we were heading back along the Siq towards the exit, we found ourselves battling against a powerful flow of arriving fellow tourists, some of them sporting garb alluding to that of Harrison Ford, and many whistling or humming the theme tune from *Indiana Jones and the Last Crusade*, the 1989 film in which he starred, for which Petra was one of the locations.

*

An *Illustrated London News* article published in March 1962 described repairs recently carried out to Al Khazna and elsewhere in Petra, and noted that 'in a poor country with a rich past, like Jordan, tourism can well form a vital element in the country's finances'. In 1985 Petra was designated a UNESCO World Heritage Site, and by 2000 the number of visitors had increased substantially. Despite a subsequent falling-off due to regional instability, numbers then rose again, and it was estimated that in 2017 some 600,000 tourists visited the site.

It is of course a real gain that more of the world's wonders can be enjoyed by more people (and without the exclusivity of the Grand Tour), but there is a real cost too, with the risk of compromising both the fabric and the character of places we set out to admire. Nor is the problem limited to sites as grand as Petra. In fact overcrowding may be especially deleterious for a smaller location. I'm thinking here of another place I love, the wonderful Doric temple of Segesta, in north-west Sicily. In the early sixties (my mother and I went there in 1963), much of the island had something of the world of *The Leopard* about it, as well as a residue of Romanticism and even of Goethe's journeying, particularly inland. Here you sensed something of ancient continuities in the rich sweeping landscapes of tilted acres, the dark spinneys and occasional ruined tower, the small towns with their cobbled streets and air of secrecy. Like Norfolk, it felt ancient.

The temple itself, first glimpsed beyond a field of springing wheat, was just there, with its perfect marching columns, its openness to visitors as much as to the sky – and not ruined, simply never roofed. Its simplicity enfolded a powerful but elusive numen.

I don't recall having to pay, though perhaps we did. I haven't been back, but I'm told that nowadays the crowds can be considerable, while access is controlled and costs. You can if you wish go on a quad bike tour that takes in Segesta along the way.

Similar problems afflict any number of popular tourist destinations, although there are places akin to Petra and Segesta, such as Assisi or Venice, whose essential nature somehow manages to outflank anything we can do to them. In the case of art galleries and museums the problem can be acute, as summer visitors to, for example, the Uffizi or the Louvre (let alone St Peter's in Rome) will know only too well. The queues can be really daunting – and with the prospect that, at the end of a wearisome wait, the visibility of what visitors have come to see may be obscured by the throng. One of the most vivid instances must be the crowds which gather at the Louvre in the hope of seeing the Mona Lisa. Said to number many thousands each day, visitors have to queue for anything between one and two hours, with only those who have booked guaranteed a sighting of the picture. As one visitor pointed out, this is in fact the third queue you have to join, after one to get into the place and another for security checks. Inevitably, when the goal is finally attained there is not much time for lingering – just long enough, said one disillusioned tourist, to take a selfie with the picture several metres away behind glass in the background. This seems more like trophy bagging, or a secular equivalent to being in the presence of a holy relic, than the chance to appreciate a work of art.

It's hard to see what can be done. At the same time, my generation of travellers ought to be properly grateful for our good fortune in having had space as well as time in which to explore. It's not just a matter of overcrowding, now that we know the need to limit our carbon footprint. Given the profligacy, environmentally speaking, of travel and particularly air travel, the future of international tourism must surely be at best an open question. And the grim challenges endured by those who travel not as tourists but as victims of persecution or disaster add their own dark shadow. The great virtues of travel remain – its capacity for broadening our outlook, extending our knowledge of the world and our capacity for fellow-feeling, together with new perspectives in which to view our own country. 'Travel makes you modest – you see what a tiny place you occupy in the world', Flaubert suggested. But it is unlikely that modesty will be enough to keep our dreams intact.

7

The jungle between two gardens

E ver since I first read *Candide* nearly sixty years ago it has been a true companion, a *vade mecum* not only of good sense but wisdom, and a source of comedy that also bears witness to human resilience. Voltaire knows only too well the dangers of blind and unconsidered optimism (*Optimism* is the alternative title he sardonically gives to his story), yet does not exclude the possibility of enduring and hoping despite everything. But this is not a lecture or a philosophical tract: a considerable part of the pleasure for readers lies in Voltaire's elegant style, and the way in which he writes with an almost offhand lightness. Where others might thump the tub, he smiles and drums his fingers.

No one has ever known better than Voltaire the art of wielding conjunctions, often to bring together two propositions which logically have nothing in common but the inconsequence of their meeting: 'since', 'because', 'hence', 'as a result', 'for' become comic devices to highlight the falsity of a given twinning, or the shortcomings of a given attitude. Thus in *Zadig*, the first of Voltaire's 'philosophical tales' to be published, the eponymous hero is known to be a man 'with great riches, and therefore with friends'; in *Candide*, the baron who owns the Westphalian château in which Candide grows up is one of the most important noblemen of the region because, we are told, his château 'had a door and windows', while his wife the Baroness 'who weighed some three hundred and fifty pounds, enjoyed as a result very considerable respect'. And Dr Pangloss, the resident tutor, assures everyone that things could not be otherwise, 'For, he said, all this is as good as it could be. For if there is a volcano at Lisbon, it could not be elsewhere. For it is impossible that things should not be where they are. For all is well.'

What exactly is meant by a 'philosophical tale'? It may sound somewhat at war with itself as a category, but it's precisely the combination of the factual and the fabulous that allows, even encourages, a satirical edge delivered with a throwaway lightness. One of the clearest definitions was that given by the critic Raymond Naves: 'In reality,' he wrote, 'These are philosophical strolls in the guise of fictional quests.' In *Candide* the quest for happiness and purpose is inseparable from that for a philosophical position able to do justice to the vagaries of the human condition and the puzzling behaviour of a god who must by definition be beneficent. A rocket of a quest, that takes off from the middle of an Edenic enclosure and has to negotiate a whole series of obstacles before coming back to earth in another garden, albeit a modest one, more refuge than paradise.

Here a whole gallimaufray of improbable actions is closely interwoven with historical events such as the Seven Years' War, the Lisbon earthquake of 1755, and the execution by the British of Admiral Byng – 'pour encourager les autres', as Voltaire famously explains. The hinterland to these fast-moving caricatures is the nature of French society of the time, grossly unequal and really threatening for anyone minded not to conform to the dictates of power. This was a culture in which the executioner would burn in public books deemed to be subversive, a sentence meted out to several of Voltaire's own works. Voltaire himself did time in the Bastille, following an altercation with an aristocrat, and at one point he was in effect exiled from Paris. It is not just in the interest of satire that the information on the title page of *Candide* declares it to have been 'translated from the German of Doctor Ralph', and purports to include 'the additions found in the Doctor's pocket at the time of his death in Minden in the Year of Grace 1759'.

It would be impossible to list all the details of the story's action without producing a flat paraphrase at odds with the buoyant style of the original, but it's worth dwelling a little on the supple opening paragraph, which quickly establishes the prevailing tone:

> There was in Westphalia, in the château of the Baron of Thunder-ten-tronckh, a young boy whom nature had endowed with the gentlest of dispositions. His physiognomy fairly indicated his soul. His judgement was quite sound, his thinking entirely straightforward; and it is for this reason, I think, that he was named Candide. The long-serving retainers of the household suspected that he was the son of the baron's sister and a good and worthy local nobleman, whom the said lady would never consider marrying because he could prove a lineage of only seventy-one heraldic quarters, and because the rest of his family tree had been lost in the ravages of time.

In the speediest of expositions we learn that the baron's idyllic household enjoys the great benefits of the tutor Pangloss (his name means 'All tongue', though 'All talk' might render it better), who holds that there is no effect without cause, allowing him to assert for instance that 'noses have been made to support spectacles, thus we have spectacles'. One day, while walking in the grounds of the château, the Baron's beautiful daughter, Cunégonde, witnesses the Doctor applying his learning to the Baroness's chambermaid, 'a very pretty and very accommodating little brunette.'

This emboldens her to pursue the attraction she already feels for Candide (as does he for her), but it takes only a dropped handkerchief and a kiss behind a screen, an incident unluckily spotted by the baron, for Candide to be kicked out, and suddenly 'all was consternation in the most beautiful and agreeable of all possible châteaux'. All this in only two pages (like all the book's thirty chapters, this first one is short), but enough to tell us that we are in for an exhilarating and hectic ride.

The world that awaits Candide on his expulsion from the earthly paradise is far from exhilarating: it's a terrible arena, a stage for all the dramas you might well associate with the worst of all possible worlds. Here armies clash with great ferocity, inflicting terrible slaughter on each other, which still allows both parties to celebrate victory with a rendering of the *Te Deum*. 'Man to man is an arrant wolf,' wrote Thomas Hobbes in *De Cive*, published in Paris in 1642, and a century later the world depicted by Voltaire seems no better. It's a place where no one is safe, where the weak find themselves entirely at the mercy of the strong, people are trafficked and women raped, and all are abandoned to the arbitrary and corrupt authority not only of temporal powers but of the church as well. Even the forces of nature seem to be arrayed against any redeeming notion of justice or mercy. Voltaire had already written a poem about the major earthquake that struck Lisbon in 1755, and here it is again in *Candide*, threatening to overwhelm the protagonists, but really there to make – with great verve – a point about the randomness of suffering and the selfishness of much of humankind. Significantly, any redeeming goodness comes from unexpected quarters. It is the non-conformist anabaptist Jacques who acts to save a brutal sailor from the sea:

> Good Jacques hurries to his aid, helps him back on board and from the effort of so doing is precipitated into the sea in full view of the sailor, who lets him perish without so much as a glance. Candide, approaching, sees his benefactor resurface momentarily before being engulfed for ever. He makes to throw himself into the sea after him; the philosopher Pangloss restrains him, by proving to him that the harbour of Lisbon had been created specifically so that this anabaptist should drown in it.

As always, Panglossian logic explains everything while comprehending nothing.

Almost throughout, *Candide* presents a relentless accumulation of cruelty, murder, concupiscence, venality and barbarism of every kind. But relief is at hand: in mid-story the reader is transported, with Candide and his loyal servant Cacambo, to the land of Eldorado, that mythical world which nonetheless several explorers had in their time set out to find. According to Candide, 'it is probably the land where all is well; for it is an absolute necessity that there should be such a country.' It is indeed an enchanted kingdom, where the visitors are welcomed by an old man of a hundred and seventy-two, who explains to them what distinguishes Eldorado from other nations – simple living; a complete absence of greed; worship of one God without the help of priests or monks; limitless hospitality dispensed by beautiful women; and, as a means of transport, flying red sheep. An audience with the king, who was to be greeted with a hug, confirms the visitors' favourable first impressions, as does a tour of the town with its elegant buildings. Moreover, when Candide asks to see the law courts,

> he was told that there was no such thing, and that people never indulged in litigation. He enquired whether there were any prisons, and was told there were not. What he found even more surprising, and afforded him the greatest pleasure of all, was the palace of the sciences, in which he saw a gallery two thousand yards long filled entirely with instruments relating to mathematics and physics.

The kingdom of Eldorado might well take its place alongside the utopias of Rabelais or Thomas More, but in the real world what place can there be for wonder or praise? The evidence to the contrary looks overwhelming. In Surinam, Candide and Cacambo encounter a slave working in the sugar refineries. 'That poor man had his left leg missing, and his right hand', the leg amputated as punishment for failed escape attempts, the hand because he caught a finger in machinery at the mill. 'This is the price at which you eat sugar in Europe, he told them.' And when Candide is tricked by the captain of a ship as well as by the judge to whom he appeals, he is overwhelmed by melancholy. 'The wickedness of men took clear shape in his mind in all its ugliness; he could feed on nothing better than sad thoughts.'

Having finally found a ship bound for Bordeaux, Candide advertises for 'an honest man willing to undertake the voyage with him, with the proviso that this man should be of all the people in the province the most disillusioned by his situation and the most wretched.' From a whole crowd of applicants Candide selects Martin, a poor scholar 'who had been robbed by his wife, beaten by his son, and abandoned by his daughter'. He is there, of course, to play for the opposition to optimism, and does so to perfection: it is Martin who dominates the final chapters, Martin who asserts that 'on surveying this globe, or rather this globule, I think that God has abandoned it to some malign being.' Candide, still nursing a weak spark of hope, wants to know why in that case the world was created. 'To drive us crazy, replied Martin.'

The rest of the tale weighs the truth of this proposition against the fortunes of the characters. The action proceeds at breakneck speed through several countries, and it takes an assortment of operatic narrative contortions to reunite the characters finally in Turkey, each with a tale of misfortune to tell. It is the pure art of caricature that has allowed everyone to survive – even Cunégonde's brother, whom Candide thought to have killed; even Pangloss, despite being hanged in Spain by the Inquisition, then 'torn to pieces, beaten black and blue', as Candide puts it, and condemned to the galleys. As for the fair Cunégonde, after all her sufferings here she is 'weathered, her eyes wrinkled, her breasts withered, cheeks lined, her arms red and flaking.' In truth, all of them are discontented and, with the exception of Pangloss, disillusioned, and Martin concludes that 'man was born to live in convulsions of anxiety, or the lethargy of despair.' Any possibility of happiness seems to have evaporated. Not altogether, though: in the final chapter, at the last gasp, two oracular encounters suggest different possibilities.

The first surfaces when Candide, Martin and Pangloss pay a visit to a local dervish, to whom they put their philosophical questions. Pangloss says to him:

> Master, we come to beg you to tell us why such a
> strange animal as man has been created. – What are

you meddling in, says the Dervish, is it any of your business? – But reverend father, said Candide, there is terrible suffering on the earth. – And what does it matter whether there is good or evil? When his Highness despatches a vessel to Egypt, does it bother him whether the mice in the hold are at their ease or not? – What then is to be done? Said Pangloss. – Keep silent, said the dervish. – I had flattered myself, said Pangloss, that we might debate together as to cause and effect, the best of all possible worlds, the origin of evil, the nature of the soul and pre-established harmony. The dervish, at these words, slammed the door in their faces.

On their way back to the smallholding where they are living, they come across an old man 'who was taking the fresh air at his door under an arbour of orange-trees'. He has found happiness by dint of never worrying about the world at large, preferring to remain outside the city while supplying it with his home-grown produce. 'You must have, said Candide to the Turk, a huge and splendid estate. – I've got just twenty acres. replied the Turk. I and my children cultivate them; work preserves us from three great evils – boredom, vice and need.'

These conversations lead on to the tale's conclusion. 'Let us work without arguing, said Martin; it is the only way to make life bearable.' And the famous closing words are those of Candide to Pangloss who, with his outlook in no way modified by experience, persists in expressing his enthusiasm for the immutable linking of cause and effect in the best of all possible worlds. 'That is well said, replied Candide, but we must cultivate our garden.'

But beyond the brilliant satire aimed at the optimism advocated by the German philosopher Gottfried Leibnitz (to which Voltaire hardly does justice, as is the way of satirists), is the story's ending really as simple as all that? Doesn't the dervish's silence, along with the sound of his slammed door, amount to the ostrich's head-burying? And what exactly is meant by Martin's 'work without arguing'? The logical consequence of his philosophical stance would seem to be fatalism: if all is for the worst in the worst of all possible worlds, how is it possible not to succumb to a pessimism as inflexible as blind optimism? This was indeed a paradox which concerned Voltaire all his life, producing different variations and emphases throughout his writings. Broadly speaking, it's a parabola that starts with the early optimism of *The Man of the World*, a poem written more than twenty years before *Candide* in which Voltaire declares, without any reservation or apparent irony, 'The earthly paradise is where I am'.

By the time of *Zadig*, published eleven years later in 1747, the earthly paradise has become the place where men are like predatory insects, and the Earth 'a little atom of mud'. In this tale (which comes much closer to

the world as experienced by Candide and his friends)
a Scythian, Babouc, is commissioned by the angel
Ituriel to decide whether the city of Persepolis should
be destroyed or allowed to survive, and to report back.
The angel's instruction is a neat encapsulation of the
scientific method: 'Go about, look, listen, observe, and
fear nothing.' As appalled by some aspects of human
behaviour as he is impressed by others, in the end
Babouc has a figurine made which incorporates both
precious jewels and base metals. Presenting it to the
angel, he asks: 'Are you going to smash this pretty
statue just because it does not consist entirely of gold
and diamonds?' Ituriel takes the point, and decides to
spare Persepolis, 'for, he said, if all is not well, all is
passable.'

But when it comes to the notion of God, human
behaviour is one thing, natural disaster quite another.
No angel can explain a phenomenon such as the Lisbon
earthquake, and Voltaire's poem about it shows signs
of sliding towards the pessimism of Martin, even if the
poem finally clings to belief of a kind :

One day all will be well, this is our hope,
All is well today, this is an illusion.

Voltaire seems to be seeking some middle way.
Fanatical as he is in the face of fanaticism, he wants
a *via medea* to fill the void between a faith abandoned

and unreason. The old man's prescription, at the end of *Candide* – to work, and so keep at bay the three great evils of vice, need and boredom, seems *bourgeois minuscule*, especially in the wake of such wanderings, sufferings and picaresque adventures. But it's of a piece with the Voltaire who, at Ferney, offered shelter and employment to refugees from the Calvinist asceticism of Geneva, and it also chimes with his reasons for admiring the mercantile traditions of the English, set out in his earlier *Lettres Philosophiques*. Of course self-interest played its part, and it would be easy to romanticize the life of this little settlement, where silk stockings and watches were made: but, like Voltaire's interventions on behalf of those persecuted after the revocation of the Edict of Nantes, it shows that the intellectual and the wit could also be an activist. As Peter Gay writes in *Voltaire's Politics* (first published in 1959, and still well worth reading), 'Ferney became a small, working instance of Voltaire's great principle— the union of free trade with free religion'.

To come back to *Candide* – as Oscar Wilde observed in *Lady Windermere's Fan*, 'life is far too important a thing ever to talk seriously about it.' In Voltaire's tale, the human condition, however hard to endure it may be, has been transformed into a soufflé of exaggeration, offering the reader an account of horrors in the tone and manner of a fairy tale. It's a bit as if someone not unlike

Wilde had rewritten the Book of Job. Since Voltaire's aim is to persuade by mockery, and to provoke, it's the language of propaganda that he wields, with all its deliberate distortions and over-simplifications. After all, 'Ecrasez l'infâme!', the great war-cry of the *philosophes* against fanaticism, is better suited to the barricades than the study. Much as Voltaire loved repeating the slogan, he also knew that the centrist position which in many ways he favoured was not an easy one to defend, any more than deism could be easily defended against the absolute of atheism.

In the world of Voltaire's *contes philosophiques*, it's not just a question of propaganda: these are the work of an expert manipulator, but also of an outstandingly accomplished writer. Time, like truth, finds itself compressed, simplified, accelerated: the tales read as if they were translations of Disney cartoons, and their protagonists share the same india-rubber ability to bounce back, whatever is thrown at them – nowhere more so than in *Candide*.

Philosophically there are distinct echoes of Pope, here and elsewhere in Voltaire's writings, and an affinity with the assertion in his 'Ode on Solitude':

Happy the man, whose wish and care
A few paternal acres bound,
Content to breathe his native air,
In his own ground.

But the gap between Pope's Arcadian vision and the Turkish smallholding where the characters in *Candide* fetch up is significant. No Edenic lustre remains: this garden is a shelter for characters traumatised by the ways of the world. What is the most important lesson that these poor people have learned? That there is no point in complaining, or asking abstract questions to which there is no demonstrable answer. Better to work than speculate; better a context of effective local action than the paralysis induced by metaphysical debate or absolutist convictions. This may be more than cold comfort, but in the story it is wisdom acquired only at a dreadful cost.

The world continues to go its way. For sure, in our own time the dervish or his descendant would have his computer and his smartphone behind the slammed door, and be as informed and impotent as we all sometimes feel. Has Voltaire's view of fanaticism and the abuses of personal and political power lost any of its pertinence? Especially now, *Candide* may serve as a reminder of the close links between entertainment – black farce, really – and power; and as a warning about the manipulation of language by those with vested interests and dubious principles. If there remain any grounds for a kind of optimism, in the form of a move towards some kind of tenable middle ground combined with radical activism, they are to be found in the persistent refusal of human beings to be discouraged, and the satirical spirit born of it. On this little atom of mud, despite the insanity of absolutist systems, there is still an abundance of compassion, goodness and mutual tolerance: proof, if not of a perfectly ordered garden, at least of a clearing in the jungle.

8

In black and white

The family got its first television set late on (and 'set' it was called, as if it were indeed in the same category as a chemistry set or a clockwork train) – to be exact, in 1961, at the midway point between the coronation (June 1953) and the moon landing on 20 July 1969. Until then, we relied on a succession of radios – the first, incorporated into a gramophone cabinet, was perhaps the most exciting of all, with the low orange lights of its valves and its red tuning needle turned to locate any one of a plethora of exotic names: Hilversum, Droitwich, Athlone, Radio Luxembourg. Its successor, a Grundig with a large green eye that showed you when it was properly tuned, was still big enough to take up most of the top of our small sideboard.

For sight rather than sound, the cinema was king. In the 1950s, even a small city such as Exeter had no fewer than three large cinemas – the Gaumont, the Odeon and the Savoy, the latter with its own mighty organ that flushed different colours as it rose smoothly out of the darkness. There were other, familial reasons that gave particular point to our interest in the cinema. My mother's brother, Basil Wright, was prominent in the British documentary film movement, as the right-hand man of John Grierson. His work had included films produced by the G.P.O. film unit, and he co-directed *Night Mail*, with music by Britten and verse by Auden written specifically for the film. An earlier film, *Song of Ceylon*, made for the Empire Tea Marketing Board, earned a place in the history of documentary. And then in the mid-1950s my mother became secretary of the Exeter Film Society, which was run by a close family friend, Stuart Keen. Long before the establishment of art house cinemas, we got to see a large number of films not distributed to the big cinema chains, including many from abroad. Later, for my generation going to the cinema was also a considerable feature of student life.

Of many films seen over the years, three have stayed with me particularly: Fellini's *La Strada* (1954), Bergman's *Wild Strawberries* (1957) – both road movies of a kind, both mixing realism with something quite other – and, from 1961, the Alain Resnais film *L'Année dernière à Marienbad*.

La Strada opens on a windy beach, where Gelsomina (the name is an Italian variation of Jasmine) is being called home by the gaggle of her four younger sisters, who tell her – 'There's a big man with a motorbike'. What follows is a brilliant exposition. Rosa, an elder sister who had gone off some time before with the man, an itinerant showman called Zampanò, is now dead. We never discover the full story, but later in the film it is implied that violence may have been involved. Now he has come back, and Gelsomina's distraught mother, caught between penury and guilt, is in effect selling Gelsomina to him for 10,000 lire.

Zampanò's character is already clear from his contemptuous air and his indifference to the family's plight. It is also clear at the outset, from her appearance and her clumsy, somewhat uncoordinated movements, that Gelsomina is a simple, childlike soul. Played by Fellini's wife Giulietta Masina, and looking much younger than Masina's thirty-three years, Gelsomina is a whey-faced girl whose thoughts and emotions are expressed not so much in words as in her eyes and facial expressions. At different times she becomes wide-eyed with sorrow or bafflement, or with joy, incredulity, wonder, delight. Her mouth, equally capable of expressing non-comprehension, excitement or a momentary sense of mischief, can crumple in grief or disappointment in exactly the way of an upset small child. She exhibits, too, a child's eagerness to please and be pleased, which is of course nothing less than the desire to be loved.

The film tells the bleak story of her life on the road with Zampanò, whose single performing act is, by the force of his powerful lungs as he says, to break free from a chain fastened tightly round his chest (an act which we see no fewer than four times during the course of the film). Gelsomina is to be his comic assistant, and to pass the hat round the audience. He kits her out with a Chaplinesque hat, a trumpet and a drum, then attempts to train her. When she initially makes mistakes, he brutally hits her with a switch taken from the branch of a tree. At night they sleep in Zampanò's bizarre wreck of a vehicle – in effect, a tricycle, with bedspace and storage built onto the back of a motorbike and covered by a rickety canvas canopy.

The action proceeds – in a cheap restaurant one evening, after his public act, Zampanò clearly has another kind in mind: he drinks heavily, then goes off on the bike with a flirty tart he has been chatting up, abandoning Gelsomina in the street. So far, so neo-realist, you think. But at that moment, as she is sitting bereft at the roadside, a large horse seen only from the rear ambles past between her and the camera – a wonderful moment and one that, along with other evidence which accumulates as the film goes on, takes the viewer closer to something like magic realism, however much the story remains firmly rooted in reality. In fact the faces and clothing of the audiences who gather to watch Zampanò, often in the open, with grim tenement blocks visible in the background in several sequences, bear witness to the struggle to get by in a society impoverished by war. They hint at a context every bit as bleak as those foregrounded in British films such as Tony Richardson's *Saturday Night and Sunday Morning* and *A Taste of Honey*. But that ambling horse suggests something more, and is only the first of a number of startling episodic developments which Fellini introduces with the utmost simplicity and skill, preparing us – appropriately, given the ramifications of the tale, for almost anything.

Together again and on the road, Gelsomina and Zampanò come to an outdoor wedding. Here a group of children, exploiting Gelsomina's simplicity, take her indoors to see a child with whom there is evidently something very wrong. Meanwhile Zampanò, like the chancer he is, chats up a careworn widow working in the household and gets her to give him her dead husband's clothes.

By the next day, Gelsomina has had enough – of Zampanò, she says, not the job. He, pitiless, makes no attempt to console her or stop her carrying out her threat to leave. She sets off to go home. While she is resting at the side of a country road, three musicians go past playing their instruments – flute, clarinet, trumpet. She follows them and is caught up in a crowd watching a large religious procession in honour of La Madonna Immaculata (this was included purely by happenstance, Fellini encountering the procession in the course of filming. Apparently the same was true of the horse that, earlier, had just strayed onto the set).

In the next sequence, darkness has fallen, and the crowd is now excitedly watching and applauding 'Il Matto', the fool, performing his tightrope act. Afterwards, clambering into his car and about to try and get through the throng, he exchanges a single look with Gelsomina. Another wonderful moment, which conveys perfectly, without words, that they have recognized something essential about each other. They know that they have in common the wisdom of the foolish and the grief of despair…In the now deserted, windy square, Gelsomina is once more sad and alone, except for a few late-night drifters. A clock strikes two. Approaching from the distance, the headlight then the rasping motor of Zampanò's bike. 'Get in!' She doesn't want to. He forces her into the back of the vehicle.

The following morning Gelsomina is roused from sleep by a donkey braying outside. They have arrived at a travelling circus where The Fool already works. Gelsomina, entranced, finds him playing a simple tune of falling notes on a miniature violin. Zampanò agrees to join the circus, and soon encounters the Fool, who provokes him with his teasing, as well as by offering

Gelsomina a role in his own act. Finally unable to tolerate the Fool when he tips a bucket of water over him, Zampanò chases him armed with a knife, and is arrested by the police. Back at the circus, Gelsomina tells the Fool that her life seems entirely pointless. But, says the Fool, 'everything serves a purpose, even a stone. If that is useless, everything is useless…' Gelsomina asks him why he had said that he would die soon. The Fool replies that one day he will fall and break his neck, and 'no one will care'. A classic archetype, then, of the joker lonely and despairing behind the bulwark of humour.

This is a key scene, but it also skates on thin ice – not only on account of the simplicity of its homespun philosophizing, but because it is a reminder of how hard it is to conjure pathos without lapsing into sentimentality: Chaplin territory, again. If Fellini succeeds in steering this tricky course, as I think he does, it is surely due to the intervention of the unexpected as well as to the superb acting not only of Masina, but Anthony Quinn as Zampanò and Richard Baseheart as the Fool.

Gelsomina and the Fool part company outside the police station where Zampanò has been held overnight: he emerges to find her and the bike waiting for him. En route to wherever they are heading next, they stop by the sea. Delighted, Gelsomina is reminded of her home along the coast; even Zampanò rolls up his trousers and wades. But when, in this moment of happiness – and fortified, too, by, the Fool's assertion that everything has a point, Gelsomina says that 'Now home seems to be with you', he responds with characteristic sarcasm.

And suddenly they are on the open road again, having acquired a nun with billowing habit and whimple as an extra passenger, crammed in alongside the showman and his assistant. Running short of petrol, they ask to spend the night at her convent. Gelsomina plays her trumpet (those falling notes again) for one of the nuns who takes a sympathetic interest in her. In the barn where they doss down for the night, with the noise of rain and thunder outside, Gelsomina tells Zampanò: 'I would even marry you.' Rebuffed. Gelsomina: 'Zampanò, aren't you a little fond of me?' No answer.

On the road once more, they come upon the Fool and his car: he has stopped to repair a puncture. Zampanò is quick to take his revenge, but in beating him up, causes him to bang his head fatally. Zampanò tries to make it look like an accident, hiding the body under a bridge and pushing the car off the road. It catches fire.

On they go, and find themselves in a cold, snowy landscape. Zampanò is seen performing his act once more, but really it's all over. Distracted, Gelsomina misses her cue on the drum and can only whimper despairingly: 'The Fool is hurt.'

The next day finds them still in a wintry landscape:

in the distance, church bells muffled by snow. They've come to a halt. For a moment, feeling the thin warmth of the sun on her, Gelsomina seems almost happy. Then she remembers: 'The Fool is hurt.' Zampanò: 'I didn't mean to kill him. I only hit him twice.' He offers to take Gelsomina home. She lies down. In a moment almost of consideration he covers her with a blanket, leaves the trumpet by her side, abandons her finally.

Time goes by. Now Zampanò is with another outfit, the Circus Medini – and with another woman, whom we see briefly as he tells her he is going for a stroll. Setting off, he is startled to hear the tune Gelsomina used to play, this time sung by children (at several points in the film, we see Gelsomina identifying with children, and this chimes with Fellini's conception of the character. 'I utilized the real Giulietta,' he wrote, 'But as I saw her. I was influenced by her childhood photographs, so elements of Gelsomina reflect a ten-year-old Giulietta.') In an exchange as deft and economical as the exposition, a young woman with the children tells him that they had learned the tune four or five years earlier, from a girl who died. The woman's father had found Gelsomina ill on the beach one evening and had brought her home. But she wouldn't eat (several times during the film she refuses food or eats only a little when told to), wasted away and died.

Now, for the last time, we see Zampanò performing

his act. It's an irony, of course, that this involves the breaking of chains and bursting free, when he is himself so firmly chained to the shortcomings of his character and by circumstances. As before, he spends the proceeds getting drunk in a bar, is asked to leave, then picks a fight with the men who have chucked him out into the street. He vents his anger by laying into some steel drums standing in the street: 'I don't need anyone. I want to stay alone.'

The film ends where it began, on the seashore, but at night. Zampanò briefly wades in, not bothering this time to take off his shoes or hoist his trousers. Staggers back onto the beach, collapses: weeps, a broken man. The wavelets roll serenely in (as they would five years on at the close of Truffaut's first film, *Les Quatre Cents Coups*).

*

Many old men do follow the advice T.S. Eliot offered in 'East Coker' and are explorers, though the area they explore is more often the expanding territory of the past rather than the diminishing zone of the future. Such is the case in Ingmar Bergman's 1957 film *Wild Strawberries*. Ostensibly the story of an elderly doctor, Isak Borg, travelling from his home to the southern Swedish city of Lund to receive an honorary degree in recognition of his services to medicine, it is a journey in which the present is shadowed – overshadowed – by memories and by a timeless world of surreal dreams. The boundaries between these zones are delineated with great skill, held apart and at the same time linked and given overall coherence by voice-overs in which Borg looks in on his life, commenting on present and past alike. His voice, sometimes gruff, often subdued, moves between wryness, regret, affection, remorse.

The success of the film owes much to Bergman's flawless interweaving of all these elements, but equally to the stunning performance of Victor Sjöström as Borg, wonderfully supported by Bibi Andersson (as Sara, his cousin and childhood sweetheart) and Ingrid Thulin (Marianne, his daughter-in-law). Sjöström, already well known as a director in his own right, was himself seventy-three at the time of filming, so that playing the seventy-eight year old Borg cannot have been entirely alien to him. All the same, he is masterly – in the subtlety with which he succeeds in conveying something close to bafflement and, at the same time, a kind of penitential view of the past. He combines being the central subject with the distancing objectivity of hovering, like Scrooge escorted by the Christmas spirits, at the margin of his own experience and assaying the past. In this the soundtrack is as important as the pictures. At the very opening of the film, before the credits, Borg is seen sitting at his desk, with voice-over conveying his thoughts; and throughout, the frequent use of voice-over provides a series of crucial links as well as giving us Borg's own estimation of past events.

The scaffolding of the journey to Lund is used to construct a memorable edifice made of scenes from the past: it's one that also houses two haunting dreams. In the first, which follows straight on from the opening credits, Borg is alone in the apparently deserted street of a brightly sunlit town. He notices a hanging clock which has no hands (but there comes the pulse of a beat which might stand for time, or equally for the beating of the heart – later, in the second dream, Borg says that he has a bad heart). He passes in front of a tightly shuttered building, and now sees a man with his back turned to him. When Borg taps him on the shoulder, he turns to show a strange face, then collapses. His fallen body leaks blood. A bell tolls. A horse-drawn hearse appears. One wheel catches the base of a streetlight, comes off, rolls away. The coffin is spilt. The lid half comes off: there is a hand sticking out which clutches Isak's wrist when he approaches. Then we see that it is Borg himself in the coffin.

It hardly seems surprising that the journey to Lund, occurring as it does in the lee of this dream, is also accompanied by other dream-like scenes from the past, notably one in which Isak's brother Sigfrid makes advances to his cousin Sara, who is picking wild strawberries in the garden of the house where they regularly spent the summers of their youth. 'I'll tell Isak', she says. The kiss: the spilled strawberries. 'What will Isak say, who really loves me?' But Isak, for whom she is intended, is seen as upright, dull, moral. By comparison, the allure of Sigrid is much more dangerous and exciting, as well as disturbing... Old Isak follows them into the house where the family is gathered for a formal lively breakfast on an uncle's nameday. Sara, upset, continues to contrast Isak's niceness with the excitement of Sigfrid. Isak, voice-over: *I was overcome by a feeling of emptiness and mournfulness.* Soon after, we learn that Sara indeed married Sigfrid, had six children and is now seventy-five.

The journey has its own incidents, not least the dialogue between Borg and his daughter-in-law Marianne, who is driving. From an initially very critical stance – 'You're an inflexible egotist', she gradually softens in her attitude to him, or rather we learn that her real criticism is directed towards the emotional coldness of her husband, Borg's son Evald, whose inability to reconcile himself to her pregnancy has resulted in their separation.

They pick up three young hitchhikers heading for Italy: Sara (played, like the other Sara, Borg's cousin, by Bibi Andersson), Viktor and Anders. The only representatives in the film of the future, their naivety and cheerfulness are depicted with affection. But then there is a near-collision with an oncoming car which swerves and overturns. Its occupants, a squabbling married couple, Alman and Berit, are unhurt. Their car is righted, but won't go, so everyone crowds into Borg's car. Alman is horrible to his wife, so much so that finally they are asked to get out of the car, and are left in the road.

The journey proceeds. Voice-over, Borg expresses mixed feelings about returning to his home area, with his nonagenarian mother living nearby. He visits her, accompanied by Marianne: his mother produces a box of children's toys, in which there is *inter alia* a pocket watch with no hands. The dream pulse starts up again. Marianne looks intently on.

They return to the car to find that Viktor and Anders, arguing about the existence of God, have resorted to fighting. When the journey resumes, Borg tells us that *I fell asleep but my sleep was haunted by dreams and images that were utterly tangible and humiliating.*

This second dream again has Borg in old age looking in on scenes from his past. It begins with a shrieking flock of birds over trees, at dusklight. We see again the basket of wild strawberries spilled. His cousin Sara holds up a mirror to him. 'I am going to marry your brother Sigfrid.' Sara runs to look after her sister

Sigbritt's baby which is lying under trees in an ornate cradle with a frilly awning. Talking consolingly to the infant, she carries it off with her. Old Isak appears, looks at the empty cradle: then is seen looking in at the window of a room where Bach is being played on the piano. Sigfrid kissing Sara. A great moon. Isak knocks on a door. The oneiric pulse starts up. True to a dream's capacity for overriding the boundaries of time, the door is opened by none other than Alman, the quarrelsome motorist, who leads Borg to a lecture theatre where a few people are sitting in banked rows of seats. Borg is subjected to a series of tests, including understanding an apparently nonsensical text on a blackboard. Alman translates and asks Borg to answer the question posed: 'A doctor's principal duty?' – Borg says he forgets, and Alman has to provide the answer, ' – is to ask forgiveness'. Borg looks over to the staring, silent audience. Alman: 'Moreover, you're guilty of guilt.' Now Borg is asked the case history and diagnosis of a patient on a couch: 'She's dead!' he concludes. At which point the 'dead' body wakes and laughs at him harshly: it is his (actually) dead wife, Karin. Alman's conclusion: 'You're incompetent'. He is also, Alman tells him, accused of callousness, selfishness and ruthlessness, charges to be brought by Karin. The pulse starts again. Now Alman and Borg are following a woodland path to a bright stage-like clearing: a seduction scene, again. Karin at first fights off her would-be lover, then submits. Alman says that Borg knows the exact day, 1 May 1917, when this happened, and 'you saw exactly what the man and woman said and did'. Karin says she will tell Isak, and predicts his pitying but cold reaction. Back to Alman and Borg, who asks: 'What will be my punishment?' Alman: 'The usual…loneliness.' Borg: 'Is there no mercy?' Alman: 'Don't ask me. I don't know about such things.' And now Borg wakes to find himself still in the car, which has stopped for the youngsters to stretch their legs.

Like the first dream, this one has abrupt twists and turns that defy daytime logic, but have psychological credibility: in many ways it is pure Kafka. It is also at the polar opposite to the purpose of his journey to Lund: not an honouring of success, but highlighting failure and humiliation. It undercuts completely the arcane academic ceremony which duly takes place when they do get to Lund, imbuing it with a sense of absurdity, a dream-like unreality of its own.

Finally reaching the end of the day, Isak thinks to see a kind of causality in it all. Under his bedroom window the hitch-hikers, about to travel on, offer him a farewell serenade. Then, as at the start of the film, we see Isak in bed. He confides that *I have a habit of recalling scenes from childhood to calm me* – and the film ends with images of a boat at a jetty in a bay, and his parents on nearby rocks, fishing: strange, distant, they wave to him. The simplicity of this, with the sense of the old man's reconciliation with his past, is particularly powerful. However much the film may be based, as is said, on Bergman's problematical relationships with his parents (his father was a Lutheran pastor), *Wild Strawberries* offers much more than that. As Bergman himself wrote (in *Images – My Life in Film*, Bloomsbury 1990): 'One thread goes through the story in multiple variations: shortcomings, poverty, emptiness, and the absence of grace.' But another thread, paradoxically, might be the fullness of old age, whatever its bleak rigours.

*

The mixed reception initially given to *L'Année dernière à Marienbad* has to some extent persisted. You can see why: the film has its flaws, among them the over-insistent organ music which accompanies much of the action (though 'action' hardly seems the right word). To some, the whole approach, the film's refusal of straightforward narrative and its passages of recurrent dialogue and monologue, seems pretentious and boring. Yet when it came out in 1961 one of its peripheral delights from the filmgoer's point of view (and perhaps especially the youthful viewer) was the way in which critics argued insistently for this or that interpretation, failing to see that the whole point is the impossibility, in the world of *Marienbad*, of any fixed linear narrative. Despite the powerful human desire to make a story of raw experience, it is precisely from exploiting this impulse by operating counter to it that the film derives its strength and character.

Within the structural outline of an unhappy love triangle of sorts, differing interpretations have swarmed – these are, it is said, characters devoid of any emotion or any psychological depth, zombies, or else robots held in a prison. The film has been criticised as too self-consciously clever, for attempting to be the story of a film being made, with a would-be *cinéaste* trying to impose his will on what happens and how – a kind of 'Three characters in search of a director'. Or else what we are watching is a story that exists in the mind of one or the other of the three protagonists; but one that is also, as the creation of the two Alains, Robbe-Grillet (who wrote the screenplay) and Resnais, a victim of its own complex layering.

It looks to be such critiques that Robbe-Grillet is

addressing in the screenplay as published, where he writes:

> Two attitudes, then, are possible: either the viewer will seek to regenerate some kind of 'cartesian' outline, of the most linear kind possible, the most rational, and such a viewer will certainly consider the film difficult, if not incomprehensible; or else on the contrary he will allow himself to be carried along by the extraordinary images he will have before him, by the actors' voices, by the noises, by the music, by the rhythm of the editing, by the heroes' passion...for this viewer the film will seem the easiest he has ever seen...

Set in a palatial hotel encrusted with embellishments, and with formally laid out grounds complete with water features and statuary, the film presents a world that is strangely oppressive and claustrophobic. The three main characters, a woman and two men, are identified only by an initial letter: the woman is referred to simply by the letter A, one of the men is X, the other M. The parts are played by Delphine Seyrig as A, Giorgio Albertazzi as X and the wonderfully gaunt Sacha Pitoëff as M, who may or may not be the woman's husband. A is svelte, elegant, often appearing distracted almost to the point of virtual absence. X is handsome, dapper, but with features that are bland, of limited expressiveness. M, tall and bony, has the kind of long face reminiscent of an El Greco figure. All three are in some way distanced: A by her introversion and evident anxiety, X by his Italian accent, M by the inscrutability of his level gaze.

The hotel has other guests – seen in couples and in groups that are static as tableaux, or else moving slowly up or down a grand staircase. At one point they are the audience for a play, at another listening to a concert, at another dancing to the slow measure of a spectral waltz. Now and again we eavesdrop on snatches of their conversation: at other times their lips move but no words are audible.

X alleges that he and A met a year before in the eponymous spa of Marienbad; that they became close, perhaps even lovers – and, on parting, had agreed to meet again a year on. A's response to this is at different times, bafflement, denial, an interest close to conceding that something may have happened, a tentative flirtatiousness, acute anxiety. M appears to shadow or control the action, continually outmanoeuvring X by looming up unexpectedly, and particularly by defeating him several times in a Nim game where the object is not to be left with the last of 16 objects (matchsticks on one occasion, cards, dominoes on others) laid out in 4 rows – of 7, 5, 3 and 1. There are other games we see being played by the hotel guests, including draughts and even pick-up-sticks, and the element of play is prominent in the whole concept of the film.

In the portrayal of the relationships between A, X and M the viewer is offered no certainty: restless possible versions of what may have occurred are presented through flashbacks, abrupt changes of location between the interior of the hotel and its grounds, and by recurrent images and words, those of X repeating his version of events in voice-over monologue. There are sequences in a shooting gallery; at a performance of a play in the hotel's theatre (a play within a play, then); in A's bedroom; close to running water in a corner of the gardens, where A allows X gently to caress her for a moment, his hand wandering down across her breast before she pulls away and in distress asks him to leave her.

At the end of the film, key questions remain unanswered. Did X become A's lover when they met in Marienbad, even perhaps against her will? Are they about to become lovers now? Has M shot A? When A finally agrees to leave with X, they are seen walking very slowly, as if hypnotized, towards the hotel entrance. Are they free agents, and where are they going? Set down like this, such questions sound arbitrary in a way the film succeeds in avoiding: in the viewer's mind, they can contribute to a powerful cumulative effect of doubt and unease.

L'Année dernière à Marienbad – the title seems

straightforwardly to give time and place, the two essential co-ordinates of lived experience. Yet it is precisely these co-ordinates that are challenged by voice and image alike, swiftly devaluing the factual data the title appears to offer. As Robbe-Grillet writes in his introduction to the screenplay, 'There is no last year, and Marienbad is no longer to be found on any map' (*Il n'y a pas d'année dernière, et Marienbad ne se trouve plus sur aucune carte.*) Though there is a Czech spa town, Mariánské Lázne, or 'Marienbad' in German, this is not it. Rather, place and time have alike been incorporated into a kind of Möbius strip, a loop of seamless recurrence in which truth is reduced to allegation, and perception to the restless mechanical questing of the camera.

From the outset, words come and go, sometimes drowned out by overbearing music, or blurred in an effect almost like radio interference, half-scrambled. Often what we hear or overhear are nothing more than what Robbe-Grillet calls '*des lambeaux de phrases*', 'shreds of sentences' which lack coherence and make it difficult to have confidence in their relevance. In X's voice-over monologues, which constitute a major element of the film, recurrences and the repetition of whole passages promote a sense of hurt or doubt, an obsessive over-insistence failing to disguise disappointment. They are also powerfully rhythmical, almost hypnotic in themselves - but more so in French than in English translation. Consider, for instance, the comparative aural effects of this:

> Et une fois de plus je m'avançais, seul, le long de ces mêmes couloirs, à travers ces mêmes salles désertes. Je longeais ces mêmes colonnades, ces mêmes galeries sans fenêtres, je franchissais ces mêmes portails, choisissant mon chemin comme au hasard parmi le dédale des itinéraires semblables.

> (And once again I was heading alone along these same corridors, through these same deserted rooms. I was going along past these same colonnades, these same windowless galleries, I was crossing the threshold of these same doorways, choosing my path as if at random among the maze of similar possible journeys.)

Here words, unreliable and obsessive as they may be, create their own imprisoning stasis, becoming an adjunct to the stifling context of the hotel. Is X trying to convince himself, as much as to tell us? As Robbe-Grillet puts it, 'The whole film is in fact the story of a winning-round: it's about a reality that the hero creates by his own vision, through his own utterances. And if his obstinacy, his secret conviction win the day in the end, it is amid such a maze of blind alleys, detours, setbacks, resumptions!'

Vision as well as utterance, then – the film relies as much on *trompe-l'œil* as *trompe-l'oreille*. From the start the camera teasingly focuses on ceilings, high chandeliers, ornamentations, as it tracks along passageways, denying us what might be visible at human height. Generally, when we are shown human figures they are immobile, intent, static: often they direct an unblinking stare at things the viewer is not always shown. The camera enacts in its own idiom the obsessiveness of X's words: again and again it noses along the hotel's corridors – with their mirrors, an engraving of the hotel grounds, the progression of the numbers on the doors along the way...Equally obsessive are gestures and stances, especially in the case of Seyrig. As suggested by Robbe-Grillet in a detailed note, A is nearly always to keep her forearm held up across her chest, hand resting on the hollow just below her shoulder, a pose that suggests defensiveness as well as a certain vulnerability. Here body language is to convey psychological characteristics more usually revealed by words and actions.

Again and again it is the camera that moves round the inert figures: this too is indicated in Robbe-Grillet's notes. For instance, 'Succession of tracking shots showing stationary characters...the camera moves round them, turns, tracks back, as if round waxwork figures in a museum. It is perhaps only the camera's movements which make their immobility seem bizarre.'

Not only mobility, but perception too is delegated to the camera. The film trades on the human desire to make sense, to be given the sense of story – here the viewers have to do the job themselves. The film's trailer goes so far as to make this explicit, exclaiming to the punter that *Vous serez vous-même le centre!* In this sense the film is a collaborative venture, in which the individual viewer must imaginatively invent any possible coherence. But to what is the viewer to give credence, and to what extent? Is there, for instance, any particular significance in the play advertised on a noticeboard being Ibsen's *Rosmerholm*, or in the playing of two string players in a concert being swamped by loud organ music?

Underlying everything is the question 'What is the truth of all this?', a question as relevant to fictional credibility as to documentary evidence. To return to Robbe-Grillet's introduction:

> In short, what do all these images amount to? They are things imagined; an imagined thing, if it is sufficiently lively, is always in the present. Memories which are 'seen again', distant regions, encounters yet to come, or even past episodes which the individual rearranges by modifying in his head and in his own time the way they were, all this is a kind of inner film continually being added to within us, the moment that we stop paying attention to what is going on around us. But at other

moments, on the contrary, we take in through all our senses that outer world so obviously there before our eyes. Thus the totality of the film in our mind embraces both sequentially and simultaneously the real fragments suggested at a given moment by sight and sound, and fragments that are past, or distant, or in the future, or entirely phantasmagorical.

This is a film set not in the indicative, the mood of narrative, but largely in the optative, the conditional or the subjunctive (defined somewhat lyrically in *Le Bon Usage* as presenting 'action as envisaged simply in terms of thought, with a greater or lesser tensing of the springs of the soul'). The grandiose context of the hotel and its décor, the geometric severity of the garden, the statuary given a prurient authority by myths and history, the intrusive assertiveness of the music – all these play off against the void of the characters' unknowability, their fixity as figures in a tableau, the stiffness of their almost-sleepwalking. It is here that X attempts to impose the logic of narrative and even of a love story on a non-narrative situation. (By the way, the music in the film, composed by Delphine Seyrig's brother Francis, does not match the suggestions in the screenplay, which envisage quite edgy and discrete serial music. Resnais has preferred the rich intensity of the organ, and in doing so risks a charge of pretentiousness.)

Unreal as this closed world is, with its robotic inhabitants, in our age of the image and with the looming development of Artificial Intelligence, this aspect of the film may fortuitously be about to gain new relevance, not least in the difficulty it highlights of defining what is properly human, along with a workable definition of truth and responsibility.

Would this film have been possible in any language other than French? The resonance of the language, so deceptive in its apparent clarity, its vocalic hum, its rhythmic onwardness – all these elements enhance the skill of the cast, and endow the film with its own sense of authority. Even Robbe-Grillet's introduction to his screenplay sounds somehow more convincing in French. But in the end, like any other film, this one must do its own work: it does so by allowing word and image to enrich one another as much in the realm of the imagination as in its representation of the physical universe.

9

Night airs

1

This is the Earth in thrall to stillness, to light. Shadows, but no secrecy; stars, but no clouds. Ecce luna, ecce terra. Here is the moon, here is the Earth that the moon has laid out for inspection. It calls for nothing but acceptance, and a thinking ahead to the old moon cradled in the new moon's arms.

2

A perfect composition. On the left, a tree where flowers are often left, in memory of an accident that happened years ago. On the right, a field full to overflowing with barley. In the centre, rising to a vanishing point, the road so invested with the moon's silver that it could be a river. And no traffic at all.

3

A time of shameless dreaming. Since dusk, the leaves of the fig, the smoke-tree and the sweet chestnut have stealthily been swelling to twice their usual size. Musk-roses and syringa, languorous, puff out their heady fragrances. An adjustment of wings in the nest half-hidden in the wall, but the birds have fallen silent. Breath caught and held. This cannot go on: sooner rather than later, the lovers' first trembling touches, clumsy with eagerness.

4

Calm Sea at Night

Darkness instinct with life
Where beacons wink like cats –
Below the horizon they seem
Soft as torchlight shone
Through skin: diffuse, precious.

Love, it must be, or at least
Seduction – the trailing trill
Of phosphorescence glinting
In the water's wicked chuckles
As it collapses into whirlpools.

Tender on the face, the wind
Blows steadily, a pressure
To be trusted, a clean whistle
Of salt, entirely innocent
Of the earth's night-time coldness.

Each masthead light parades
Its triumph of pride across
The viscous, quickening sea
Where all engines turn
In a self-forgetting sleep.

And the moon, when at last it breaks
Free from the trawling clouds
Can do nothing, pale and swollen
As it is, but carry over
Our dreams to the coming dawn.

5

The indolence of the south: it doesn't matter where. Only
that it is still hot, long after the sun has set. On the chalk
paths, lizards and snakes have left their marks: glowworms
twinkle in the low grassy bank along one side of the vineyard.
The cicadas persist, their obliggato as dry as seasoned wood.
There is a limpness to the trees, even the short sturdy olives.

High in the soaring poplars, the night breeze is shaking its tambourines.

6

The ripening apples are starting to weigh, to weigh down the branches of the old trees in the orchard. The night dew glistens on their blossoming skins. Underfoot, the earth has gathered into mounds.

10

From early morning to late twilight

I n 2005 the British Museum put on a major Samuel Palmer exhibition, chronologically arranged and so comprehensive that to visit it was to gather a vivid impression of the life as well as the work. Here were the small pictures from the years spent at Shoreham, in Kent, in his twenties; the much larger landscapes of his middle years, some showing Devon and Cornish scenes, many the fruit of his time in Italy; and the late work, with its return to a more modest scale, and closer to the spirit of his early paintings.

About to leave the final room of the exhibition, I and the friend with me, Penelope, circled back to enjoy the Shoreham pictures once more, in particular the six executed in brown ink and sepia mixed with gum arabica, which I had first seen at the Ashmolean in Oxford some years before. It was hard to believe that from such a striking start – he was only nineteen or twenty when he painted them – Palmer could have gone on to produce work on such a epic scale, much of it really little more than competent. There were understandable reasons for such a change of course, financial considerations among them: but it was still a shock to compare the basic lifelessness of the big pieces with the exceptional intensity of the Shoreham sepias, an intensity enhanced by the medium. The addition of glue to the ink and sepia makes for a rich layering and produces an atmospheric glow of light that the big set pieces lack completely.

It's not entirely certain what order the sepias were produced in, but given their titles (not all of them original) it makes sense to think of them as a kind of sequence running through the day. Certainly it would be hard to imagine a more invigorating start than *Early Morning*. The left side of the picture is dominated by a great tree the shape of a darning-mushroom, its energetic curve linking it to the swooping hillsides and the cottage in the centre background, with its eyebrow thatch. Even the artist's signature has a rainbow curve to it. Like all six sepias to a greater or lesser degree, the composition combines the circular and the triangular.

It's worth remembering that these are small pictures, about 18 by 24 centimetres: as *Early Morning* demonstrates, there is nonetheless an extraordinary amount of detail for the eye to take in. The grass, tree foliage and plants have real luxuriance: here everything is abundant and flourishing, especially the wheat-crammed field at the centre. You won't necessarily spot at once the four figures sitting in front of the crop, at the junction of two falling slopes, tucked in as neatly as a handkerchief into a breast pocket. Seemingly a family group, it calls to mind Palmer's oil painting, in just such a pastoral context, of the holy family resting on the flight from Egypt. Beyond the tree, casting brightness and shadow across its trunk and branches, the sun is already high enough to radiate an intense shimmer. And, undisturbed by the presence of humans nearby, alone on the path running diagonally back and up from left to right in the foreground, a single hare is snuffing the morning. On the right, the pillars of four more tall trees. To the left, lying alongside the path, a large solid log.

A Rustic Scene, conceived as an illustration for a scene in Virgil's *Georgics*, shows similar features. To left, right and centre lie three hills, steep and rounded enough to look like tors: and here too, the centre of the picture is a crammed field, foreshortened so that the tall stems and bulging ears of the crop look over-large. In the foreground, it would be easy to miss the swooping hill-slope which is actually the thatch of a cottage almost completely blocked out by the bulk of an ox that a ploughman is in the process of yoking. The ox is massive, and its tough curly fleece exemplifies Palmer's gift for rendering texture. Yet, considerable as it is (and it wouldn't seem out of place alongside a Michael Ayrton minotaur, or a Henry Moore figure), the beast is assimilated, halfway to being concealed, by the surrounding landscape. Come to that, even the ploughman's boater-shaped hat has a textured pattern that melts into the shadowed slope of the field behind him.

Only two of the six pictures have no fields with crops, and *Valley with a Bright Cloud* is one of them. To the left, a steep tipping field combed into furrows; front right, a rich splay of arcing leaves. In the centre and halfway back, one of Palmer's characteristic groups of trees. The sky looks windy, with a great blossoming cloud that catches the viewer's eye at once. As in *Early Morning* there is a log on the ground – but here looming larger and more darkly. The valley itself, with a church spire and a dwelling, is barely discernible in its shady occlusion. Even now you may not have noticed the colloquy of a pair of birds on the ground at the bottom of the picture, or the three miniscule creatures to be glimpsed on a distant hilltop beyond the trees.

By comparison, *The Valley Thick with Corn* seems at first a much more open landscape, and though it includes many of the same features as the other pictures, they have been re-arranged and are much more than stage props – the log has become an upright stump; the path is less prominent, winding steeply away into the distance; some of the crop, harvested, leans together in stooks. But there are new details, too – two cows, one black and one white; a shepherd playing his pipe, some of his flock lying down, others lapping from a small pond nearby; with, in the background, a diminutive house, and a horse, cart and driver toiling up the flank of a great hill. At the centre, two cottages seem trapped in a swirling vortex of trees…And then, the bearded figure reclining, propped on his left elbow, immersed in his book, his absorption a reminder of the way in which all these landscapes have an inwardness alongside the world of appearances.

The second of the pictures not to sport a field with crops is *The Skirts of a Wood*. Here the figure of a piping shepherd is foregrounded, sitting against the trunk of an enormous chestnut tree. The sheep, lying at ease nearby, look suitably lulled. More than any of the other pictures this one emphasises the denseness and complexity of trees and bushes, evidence of the close observation of nature that Palmer advocated. One tree has a wrenched trunk, another a low, swollen bole; a birch displays its horizontal lenticels. At the back, a glimpse of distant dwellings at the end of a swerving track. Steep hillsides have become peripheral, barely glimpsed at either side: on the right, a second, tiny shepherd is leaning on his crook by his sheep, standing close to the edge of a sheer drop. And woven into the texture of the chestnut's leaves and branches is a large oval nest, where parent birds are warding a fine clutch of eggs. And is that another cottage half-hidden on the right?

Of all the titles given to these pictures, *Late Twilight* is perhaps the one Palmer aficionados will most readily identify with, recalling pictures such as *The Flock and the Star* and others too, in which the moon presides over soft mounds of slumbering sheep. Here, slopes lead up to the apex of a haloed moon lifting above a stand of tall trees, the triangular rising to the circular. Many of the typical Palmer features are present – log, rabbit (or hare?), sheep, an uncertain figure beyond a gate, a church with its roof glinting in the moonlight, the corn bound and standing in stooks, one distant house on a ridge and another in the lee of a hill. The sky is seen as a horizontal layer of low cloud with, above, the impending dark.

*

Palmer's reputation, both during his life and since, has not been altogether straightforward. Given his known dislike for the new art of his own time, his membership of the group calling themselves (almost defiantly) 'the Ancients' and his capacity for voicing reactionary political views, this is not altogether surprising. He also had a tendency to produce prolix and preachy verse.

Like Blake, whom he greatly admired, he disliked what he saw of city life as it was then developing. His art was dismissed by some as old-fashioned, by others as incompetent or merely nostalgic. Yet he has been more fortunate in recent times, with apologists such as Geoffrey Grigson and Raymond Lister, both champions of the Shoreham work.

Palmer's own later allusions to the years at Shoreham seem to have been sparse enough, and when he does refer to them it is to weigh them critically against his sense of a 'loftier vision'. On one level this can be seen as an unresolved tussle between faith and a sense of his own shortcomings, articulated and perhaps revealed more than he realises by a sometimes perfervid piety: but in a letter written to his wife Hannah from Hastings in the summer of 1859 in a mood of dejection, he confesses quite straightforwardly that 'I seem doomed never to see again that first flush of summer splendour which entranced me at Shoreham.' However, writing in November 1871 to Frederic Stephens, a founder of the Pre-Raphaelite Brotherhood, his happy memories are qualified:

> Forced into the country by illness, I lived afterwards for
> about seven years at Shoreham, in Kent…the beautiful
> was loved for itself, and if it were right, after any sort,
> to live for our own gratification, the retrospect might be
> happy…

The same note of implied dissatisfaction is struck in a letter about his engraving *The Bellman* to the art critic and novelist Philip Hamerton, written in August 1879:

It is a breaking out of village-fever long after contact – a dream of that genuine village where I lost, as some would say, seven years in musing over many strings, designing what nobody would care for...

Some of the notes in Palmer's 1824 sketchbook show that this quarrel with himself about the gap between the artist's observation of the natural world and the urge to insist on a Christian or Platonic context started early. He always writes with much more direct enthusiasm about what he actually sees: and here, in a letter written from Shoreham in December 1828 to the artist John Linnell, he seems to want to negotiate between these two levels of perception. 'General Nature', he writes, 'is simple and lovely', and has claims of its own to make, even alongside the 'loftier vision' described in the sketchbook:

However, creation sometimes pours into the spiritual eye the radiance of Heaven: the green mountains that glimmer in a summer gloaming from the dusky yet bloomy East; the moon, opening her golden eye, or walking in brightness among innumerable islands light, not only thrill the optic nerve, but shed a mild, a grateful an unearthly lustre into the inmost spirits...

Perhaps this perceived gap between the visual and the visionary is to some extent illusory: what impresses me most of all about the Shoreham sepias is the inwardness of the natural world they depict, in all its radiant and lovingly observed beauty.

In any case, the particular achievements of the Shoreham period were not to recur. Following the death of his much loved son Thomas in 1861 (his daughter Anna had already died at the age of three, in 1847) Palmer did return to something closer to his earlier style and subjects, but such works as the well-known engraving *The Lonely Tower* lay the emphasis, as the title suggests, on solitude and isolation. His move away from the youthful pictures that posterity was to promote occurred long before grief took him somewhere near to them again. It is as if he was too distracted by the conflict between devotion and dubiety, or simply too young, to realise how far he had already gone towards fulfilling his gift.

11

Private views

The Museum Berggruen in Berlin stands opposite the grand buildings and grounds of Schloß Charlottenburg. I was last there on a bright Sunday morning in August 2019. I arrived as the gallery opened: its solid, quite narrow door looked more like the entrance to a government office than the threshold of an art gallery. But once beyond it, up a few steps, you have only to buy and show your ticket – and there she is, waiting for you. She stands nearly seven feet tall, beneath a fine rotunda through which the light streams in overhead. The black bronze of her body is heavily worked. Her shoulders are square and narrow. Her breasts sag. She keeps her arms and hands held in to her sides. Her feet are so close together that they seem almost to melt into one another, and into the small oblong base on which she is standing. On her extraordinarily thin stem of a neck, the precariously perched head looks very small. The features are delineated just enough for you to see that her mouth is downturned, her eyes somewhat sunken.

In a nearby room, you can watch a video that includes a scene with an elderly gentleman standing exactly at the foot of the rotunda, where there is nothing more to be seen than an empty space. He spreads his arms, and exclaims with great enthusiasm that of course this is where it must go: this has to be the place for it.

Tall Nude Standing III, bronze, 1960, a small plaque on the wall tells you. But its title cannot convey the powerful character of this sculpture by Alberto Giacometti. It is not easy to describe its impact exactly. A strong element of pathos inheres in it, and a sense of isolation, though Giacometti insisted that it was not his intention to depict loneliness. Nor, he said, did this figure and others like it refer to the victims of Second World War concentration camps, as some had suggested. Historically, it has clear links with the kind of figurines and statues made by the Etruscans, whose home ground in Volterra Giacometti had visited, excitedly seeing when he did so one of the most impressive of their creations, known as *The Evening's Shadow*. The hieratic stance of Giacometti's woman is also a reminder of his interest in Ancient Egyptian statues – those arms held in, the feet as if half mummified in the bandaging of their togetherness.

Giacometti tended to say that he knew very little about anything, including his own work – that it was all a mystery to him. When you read about Giacometti's life, it certainly seems mysterious, if not miraculous, that he was able to navigate the quarrelsome factions and shifting allegiances of his surrealist fellow artists and writers and then, having parted company with them, to find his own way. That wasn't easy either – in the late 1940s he found that his sculptures were (again, in a way he said he could not help but didn't fully understand) getting smaller and smaller, figurines no taller than 27 centimetres at most. And then, improbably, he works his way through to figures on a vastly greater scale, even if they retain something of the delicacy and minimalism of the earlier sculptures.

Sixty years on, it may after all be almost impossible for the viewer not to look at *Tall Nude Standing III* through the prism of what we know only too well – the emaciation of the starving, the deprivations of prison camps. Even so, this cannot entirely account for the fascination that the figure exerts. There is something else going on here, and I don't think I would have understood what it is without the staircase which coils round the sculpture and rises through the first and second floors. When you go up, as you are free to do, the changing angles offer a developing perspective. Climbing the turning stair, you see that she seems less monumental than you had initially thought when on the ground floor, looking up at her. The narrowness of the shoulders, the slenderness of the neck and the precariousness of the head are all more noticeable. When you look down at her from the second floor, the overwhelming impression you have is of a human fragility and diminishment that seem to demand protection.

In a sense her protector was the man seen waving his arms in the video, who had decided so brilliantly on placing her in the rotunda. He was the art dealer and collector Heinz Berggruen, after whom the gallery is named. Fleeing from Germany to America in 1936 in his early twenties, Berggruen studied German literature at Berkeley, then worked as an art critic for the San Francisco Chronicle before getting a job at the city's Museum of Modern Art. He returned to Europe after the war, settled in Paris and built up a formidable collection over the years (the first picture he bought, in 1940, was a watercolour by Klee). In 2001 Berggruen estimated the value of his collection as $450 million: by then it included 165 works by 20th-century artists, notably Picasso, Klee, Matisse and Braque, as well as Giacometti. In 1996 Berggruen, born and brought up in Berlin, agreed to lend his collection for display here in the West Stüler building, and four years later it was acquired for the Nationalgalerie of the Staatliche Museen zu Berlin. Four years after that the building was renamed the Museum Berggruen, in celebration of his

94th birthday, and in 2007 – by which time the collection included many additional loans and acquisitions, the museum premises were extended by the incorporation of the neighbouring Kommandantenhaus, and the two buildings connected by an elegant covered passage at ground floor level.

The enlargement has been brilliantly executed, enabling the gallery to retain its essential intimacy. The layout is quite labyrinthine, with the collection displayed over three floors in a series of small rooms – four or six of them at each level – leading off from the hub of a central landing. Many of the rooms contain no more than three or four pictures, with a generous amount of white wall space around them: some have a quotation from a text or lecture by the artist in question. A number of the rooms have a very simple bench of polished wood in the middle, others a black wrought-iron chair tucked into the angle of a corner, intended perhaps for staff rather than visitors. There is a plainness about it all that guarantees a complete absence of any distraction, and maximum focus on the pictures and sculptures on display. Drifting from one small room to the next and the next gives the visitor a great sense of leisurely discovery, as well as the feeling that the ten Euros it costs to get in is astonishingly reasonable.

I've always loved Paul Klee's paintings, and certainly

the number and quality of those in the Berggruen Collection (Klee's earliest paintings, along with those of the 1920s, are particularly well represented) make this one of the gallery's highlights. Yet the excitement of that Giacometti figure at the entrance gives it a memorability all of its own: and its impact is enhanced by the contrast with other Giacometti works exhibited – the five small figures in motion (all less than an inch or so tall) of *The Square*, as well as the wonderful *Cat* displayed on a high shelf in one of the rooms in the extension. Its head and tail reach beyond the solid base on which it stands, and its body is of a skeletal thinness which makes the identity of its creator unmistakeable. It is as horizontal in its thrust as the standing woman is vertical, and probes the air, sniffing at the way forward.

I'm still thinking, though, about the standing woman: the way in which she seems so far off, reminding me of a Masai I once sighted on a distant ridge in Kenya. Yet she is close too, looming up just in front of you. Here, and in a different way in his smaller figures, Giacometti has succeeded in doing something really unusual: paradoxical as it may seem, he has combined in one figure the long view of distance with the immediacy of close quarters.

*

In the same year that Heinz Berggruen left Berlin to go

to America, another art collector and friend to artists, Jim Ede, abandoned England in favour of Morocco. He had studied at Newlyn Art School, then served in the First World War with the South Wales Borderers and the Indian Army, before ill-health caused him to resign his commission. After continuing his studies at the Slade School of Art, he got a job at the Tate Gallery in London (then called the National Gallery of British Art). He wanted especially to promote the work of contemporary artists, among them Picasso and Mondrian, but too often found himself coming up against the cautious conservatism of his superiors. So frustration played its part in his decision to go and live in Morocco.

There followed twenty years of travel in Europe and America, lecturing and broadcasting while keeping his Moroccan house outside Tangiers – until 1952, when Ede and his wife Helen moved to France, and a house near Amboise in the Loire Valley. Returning to England in 1956, they were on the lookout for a building worthy of housing their by now considerable art collection. In the event, they bought and converted four somewhat tumbledown cottages at Kettle's Yard, in Cambridge.

The present-day visitor can see what they made of their acquisition. To the right of the closed door, there is a bell with a rope to be pulled. You have only to ring and, after a short pause, someone will appear to let you in. On entering, you discover that you seem to have walked into someone's home. You find a sitting-room, then (tucked into an alcove by a large chimney breast) there is a dining table with chairs, beyond that a bedroom and a bathroom. On the first floor, more rooms to explore and, up a further narrow staircase, an attic. In addition, a two-floor extension was added in 1970.

By the time you leave you will have discovered just how remarkable Kettle's Yard is, and how hard to categorise. As Jim Ede was keen to emphasise, it is not a museum. You can see that – what museum is as free of labels and explicatory text as this place? Nor is it, quite, a gallery. How many galleries are adorned with fresh flowers in almost every room, or hang their pictures in such domestic settings, including a bathroom and lavatory?

The pictures themselves add up to a remarkable account of the earlier 20th century British avant-garde, bringing together the hieratic obliquities of David Jones's multi-layered paintings and calligraphy, Henri Gaudier-Brzeska's drawings and sculptures (among the best of these is a dynamic bronze cast of *A bird swallowing a fish*), Ben Nicholson's explorations of space and light, Winifred Nicholson's delicately coloured flower paintings, Christopher Wood's seascapes, including a dynamic view of a Breton boat under construction and a bold self-portrait. There are many striking paintings by Alfred Wallis, the self-taught Cornish fisherman who took up painting as a consolation after the death of his wife, and whose work appealed so much to the Nicholsons and Christopher Wood. His sailing boats and trawlers, colourful and depicted with an almost childlike directness, pitch through seas where submerged fish loom like lost souls, or are seen against the flattened-out background of a harbour, a lighthouse, a row of houses.

There are not only pictures and sculptures, but also ceramics, furniture and books, with a library on the first floor where visitors have the opportunity to sit and read – and everywhere, vases of flowers, never overblown, entirely without panache, more like posies gathered on an afternoon walk than anything more formal. There is so much to take in and that claims your proper attention – the grain of wood on a chest or table, the shapes, colours, and texture of pebbles arranged here and there in a coil of punctuation, the natural stone complementing the polished energy of the worked stone of sculptures.

All this is in keeping with Ede's firmly held convictions about the importance of art in the totality of its relation to nature and to life generally. He did not want his collection to be simply the evidence of one man's preferences or to reflect only 'the taste of a given period', but rather 'a continuing way of life'. For him the conjoining of the worlds of art and of experience was seamless: one positive expression of this was his readiness to invite university students to come to tea and look round the collection, and even to borrow paintings to hang in their rooms during term-time. With the same kind of generosity as that shown by Heinz Berggruen, in 1966 he gave the house and collection to the University.

At Kettle's Yard you wander freely at your own pace, and begin to see how much the effect of the place relies on the totality that it presents. Everything here is of a piece, even the most separate part of the house, the attic. (Its warm gloaming is like a shed in summer and, though it is just under the roof, it also has the deep-down sense of somewhere below deck in an old wooden ship.) All that you see belongs together, in associations of light and shadow and the context of a space that, once lived-in, remains living. Within this integrity, there is an honouring of each object in its singularity, in the quiddity of each constituent part: yet nothing is roped off, or made into a precinct.

The lives of the artists whose pictures, sculptures and books make up the ensemble bear witness to their share of human struggle: think of Henri Gaudier-Brzeska, killed at Neuville-Saint-Vaast in 1915, or Christopher Wood, going under a train at Salisbury station at the age of twenty-nine. Yet there is nothing elegaic in the atmosphere. The empty chairs, the china no longer used, the divan bed no longer rumpled by use, the two baby grand pianos – all are free of ghosts, keeping a sense of the actual and the everyday that museum-pieces rarely manage to retain. It's remarkable, too, that the extension to the house succeeds in remaining true to the substance as well as the tone and scale of the original cottages – which must be due largely to the fact that Jim and Helen Ede continued to live there until 1973.

Return visits always bring to your attention something you hadn't noticed before – a glass vase, a rug, a picture, the interplay of light and shadow at a given point: and always there is the freedom of being able to make of it all what you will, without the indicative guidance of labels or text. Each visit becomes, in its own way, a progress that might be said to mirror what Robert Frost wrote in 'The Figure a Poem Makes' – one that 'begins in delight and ends in wisdom'. Or at any rate the beginnings of wisdom, in understanding what Jim Ede meant when he talked of 'a continuity of enjoyment'. That notion of continuity is something well worth taking with you as you head back into the world outside.

Like the Berggruen Collection, Kettle's Yard shows how relevant context is to the ordering of our perceptions. Both places – the plain minimalism of the Berggruen Museum, the domestic richness and careful placements of Jim and Helen Ede's house – invite us to consider the question of value in art, and therefore also in life. Both are remarkable public places that encourage us to define our private views.

12

Sea-horse

Slowness has brought the reward of grace, and an aura of dignity. He rises and falls in a state of grace.

He is not toppling, but nodding forward, or bowing. Sometimes he will drift downwards from his own tail, after tethering it to sea-grass, coral or a sponge.

He looks to be old, and more like a chess piece or some other wooden carving than a sea creature.

His colours, encrusted, are silver-green-grey. He can change them if he likes.

When he moves forward, it can be a wonder of verticality.

The little arms of his side fins and the frill of the dorsal one suggest incredibly fine tuning, the potential for skilled mid-course corrections even when he is heading for nowhere in particular.

The question mark is his heraldic emblem, but he can also curl into an O.

His snout calls for a bridle, his boxy mane for a brush.

His delicacy doesn't prevent him from containing multitudes.

But of real time he knows nothing.

13

Bach, Brahms and the big end

The scene is a field in a valley somewhere on the fringe of the Mendips, on a summer evening in 1959. A grey Rover 90 is parked by the gate. Sitting awkwardly on a rug spread on the grass, two boys from the same school boarding house: on another rug, their housemaster and his housekeeper. She unpacks a fine picnic that includes chicken drumsticks and appetising red nuggets of strawberries. But the real treat is yet to come: this quartet is on its way to Wells Cathedral, to hear Yehudi Menuhin and his orchestra play all six Brandenburg Concertos in a single concert.

Such an outing was characteristic of the generosity of my housemaster, Laurence May. As far as I know he didn't himself play an instrument or sing, but music was an important centre of his life, to the extent that every so often he would risk exposing the junior boys in the dayroom to a selection of classical music on LPs. Sitting in close rows on stiff-backed chairs, the audience would display reactions varying from laconic tolerance to pained weariness: it certainly wasn't considered cool to show enthusiasm. One or two cleaned their C.C.F. cap badges or tried to read a book under cover of the person sitting in front of them, thus risking punishment. Laurence May must have realised that a fair percentage of the listeners was agog with indifference, but he persisted gamely, even giving a short introduction to each item in his shy, red-faced manner. His selections included Respighi's arrangement of Rossini's *La Boutique Fantasque*, and he must have thought this hit the spot because it almost always featured, so that it was more or less a signature tune, to be anticipated and greeted with derision. As I recall, other choices included, optimistically, Mozart and Schubert string quartets and the 'March to the Scaffold' movement from Berlioz's *Symphonie Fantastique*, as well as Ravel's *Boléro* and *The Sorcerer's Apprentice* by Paul Dukas. You could see where he was coming from. There may even have been an extract from one of the Brandenburgs.

The picnic ended a bit earlier than necessary, due to the mildly comic arrival of some cows reluctant to be shooed away, but it was the music that made the evening properly unforgettable, its impact enhanced by the setting of the cathedral with its exquisitely painted nave ceiling and the extraordinary scissor arches which, though looking entirely modern, were fourteenth century additions to support the central tower. But those Brandenburgs! There was so much that was simply thrilling, not least the highlights of the trumpet in the second concerto and the harpsichord in the fifth. I think of the whole occasion as one of the markers accounting for my lifelong wonder at Bach's music. It's impossible to make any kind of excluding choice from among all those choral, orchestral and instrumental works: but what comes through to me overall from his stupendous output is a remarkable faith in life, a belief in sense and shape so sturdy and joyous as to be unshakeable, whatever the vicissitudes of existence. His work achieves a universality that outgrows, as well as growing out of, the Lutheran base from which he operated.

I shall, after all, risk one or two particular choices: the motet *Fürchte dich nicht, ich bin bei dir*; the *Goldberg Variations*, preferably played by András Schiff (I was lucky enough to hear him perform them at a 2015 Prom); and the six Cello Suites (*Suites à Violoncello Solo senza Basso*, to give the title on the cover of the manuscript). There is something hugely appealing about the cello as an instrument. Its expressive range is extraordinary, from the pent emotion of its higher notes to the ruminant reflectiveness or the boisterousness (it can do either equally well) of the lower ones. There is a kind of expressiveness, too, in the physical relationship between instrument and player: the intimacy of a near embrace, an attentive bending forward. The Cello Suites are excellent demonstrations of the instrument's possibilities. I have a particular liking for the recordings (no fewer than five of them, over more than forty years) made by the Hungarian-born János Starker: the LPs that I once had and the CDs which replaced them have in common that they are recorded very close to, which produces real bite and highlights both the joyful liveliness of some of the movements and the contemplative depth of others. One of the latter that I love best is the fourth movement of the fourth suite:

Sarabande

In the rich sparseness
of late winter
time slows
to a lull going
nowhere, nearly

It is like a trance
induced by knowledge,
or an intimate love
always shadowed
by its counterpoint

Deep into summer
it will stay, this stopped

ground – as if leaves
could remain locked
in the sappy branches

Will stay as a dream
with nothing forgotten
even where the path
rises to sunlight
and airy silence

*

As a plan for an outing it didn't seem wildly ambitious. Four of us, all living in the enchantment of 1963, our second (and exam-free) year at Oxford, would drive down to London to a concert. I had an LP of Clifford Curzon playing the Brahms 1st Piano Concerto in D Minor, recorded the year before at the Kingsway Hall, with George Szell and the London Symphony Orchestra: the dapper figure of the soloist shown on the cover had him posing by the piano, considering the score with an apparent casualness that completely belied his thrilling account of the music. Now, by an extraordinary stroke of luck, here he was in London once more to perform the Concerto at the Royal Festival Hall, again with the London Symphony Orchestra, but this time under the baton of Pierre Monteux, by then in his late eighties.

We set off on a sunny May afternoon, taking the road south to Henley and picking up the M4 close to Maidenhead. Somewhere near Slough, with a bang worthy of a Brahms drumroll, the elderly VW we were travelling in decided it had had enough. From here on, the plot development seemed more suited to opera than orchestra. Given that this was well before the era of mobile phones, I think one or more of us must have hitch-hiked to Heston Services, and somehow managed to get a taxi to take us back to the VW, and then all four of us on to London. At that point the opera turned comic, with one of us (sitting in front) mistakenly thinking that we had been saved not by a taxi but by a good Samaritan. His expressions of thanks to the driver were effusive but misplaced, and when we reached the Festival Hall we had to hand over most of the money we had on us. In the concert interval Graham, one of our number, was able to summon further help in the person of his father – his parents lived at Eastcote, near Pinner. Astonishingly, with a nobility understandably tempered by irritation, and his temper moderated by the presence of his wife (who had accompanied him with that express intention), Graham's father met us at Baker Street after the concert and took us back to Oxford. I hope we told him adequately how grateful we were.

Curzon's playing was every bit as exciting as we

had thought it would be. The power and subtlety of his performance, already clear from the LP, was greatly reinforced by hearing it live, with sight added to sound. He was a completely unshowy player, apart from his tendency to lift himself several inches off the stool at moments of particular emphasis or drama. You felt that he was entirely at the service of the music, wonderfully able to articulate the marked contrasts of its detail while never losing his sense of the overall structure. So much of the First Concerto relies for its forcefulness on the interplay of the intensely dramatic and the intimately lyrical, and perhaps it is that which made it so appealing to us at the age we were – close to the age at which Brahms began work on the concerto, which he completed after five years, when he was twenty-five.

The opening of the first movement (aptly designated *Maestoso*) could scarcely be more theatrical, with its ominous chords and loud drumrolls: yet this is soon taken down to a quietly reflective passage, only for this to lead to a return of the opening statement, then the soloist's first entry, a series of restless trills taken up by the orchestra. Here and throughout, the relation of the piano part and the orchestra to one another is fascinating – the way in which either, preceding or following the other, not only establishes a dialogue but produces a seamless linking (often enacted by the woodwind, oboes, clarinets and flutes), while at the same time the contrasting moods and voices remain distinct. Nowhere is this more manifest than at the point in the first movement where the drama gives way to a wonderful clarification, the sound of a horn as if in the deep distance. It's a figure that always reminds me of the telling final line of Vigny's poem 'Le Cor', about Roland at Roncevaux: 'Dieu! Que le son du cor est triste au fond des bois.' You could say that in some respects the whole concerto plays off the depth of distance against the immediacy of close-up, the two subsumed in an overarching development that alternately advances and retreats.

The calm repose of the second movement (*Adagio*) also begins with an orchestral passage – but this time poised, almost elegiac: and the piano entry, when it comes, is beautifully simple and lyrical. Curzon played it with a limpidity that recalled his love of Mozart. It builds slowly: soft horns, woodwind, hushed strings. Remarkably, many of the piano passages seem almost tentative, provisional: loose arpeggios that wander dreamily as if in search of the way forward, until they swell gently to a momentary reconciliation with the orchestra. The effect is hypnotic and this pattern, repeated and culminating in a series of fluttering trills, articulates an intensity that is always aware of silence at its back.

At the start of the third and final movement (*Rondo: Allegro non troppo*) the piano plunges straight in, with a vigour enough to jerk you upright in your seat – a brisk dance with a lively sense of drama, but markedly less melancholic than the mood of the first movement. Closer to playfulness than anything so far, it comes at you in waves, with now the soloist, now the orchestra leading the way. The pace quickens, culminating in an extended piano cadenza. Then, an echo of those woodland horns before a final gathering. If the concerto ends on a note of resolution rather than triumph, that seems true to the tensions underlying the work.

The concert ended with a work none of us had heard before, the César Franck Symphony, also in D Minor and, like the Brahms, a work received with a notable lack of enthusiasm by its first audience. It swept us along, from the sombre opening to the uninhibited verve of the last movement – the kind of exultant writing for brass that you might associate more with a swing band than an organist. It was exhilarating stuff, and very nearly enough to protect us from the evening's downbeat coda. The car, having failed to deliver us, really had had it, its big end gone and the engine having imploded. Without us knowing it at the time, before ever we got to the concert the Volkswagen had performed its own *German Requiem*.

14

Tools of the trade

T he kind of school desk I have in mind is something you might now find in an antique shop. Extremely heavy, probably made of oak, it incorporated a seat with a back to it as well as the actual writing surface: it seemed like a self-contained vehicle of some sort, an impractical kind of sledge. When you lifted the lid, there was a cavernous space with plenty of room for books and stationery – though under a slew of these you might well have found an accumulation of litter, sweet and bubble gum wrappers, an odd marble or two, the remains of last season's conkers, twists of wood shavings from a pencil sharpener. At the front edge of the desk, just beyond the lifting lid, there was a slight indentation designed to hold a pen with, on the right, a white china inkwell in which to dip it. The pen itself was a simple wooden shaft onto which you clipped a metal nib. New nibs worked best when wetted with spittle before you began to write.

From today's perspectives, such equipment is almost

as remote as Babylonian clay tablets, but it isn't so long ago that a post of some importance among schoolchildren was that of ink monitor. He or she, usually easy to identify by the amount of ink that had worked its way into the pores of the skin, was responsible for checking the supply of ink and ensuring the inkwells were full. Inevitably a fair amount of ink found its way onto clothing and into books: for tidy work and exams, blotting paper ('blotch') was essential. It was treated as a rare commodity and doled out parsimoniously, one pink or white rectangle per pupil. It used to remind me of historical films in which, presumably in an attempt at accurate detail, the writer of a letter would shake a large pepperpot filled with sand over a just completed letter, before rolling up the parchment. No blotch then.

School ink had a character of its own. Blue-grey in colour, it had to be reconstituted from powder, a process akin to the miraculous liquefaction of the blood of a saint. If diluted too much, it would issue in a pale hue which looked already faded and quickly faded more – good news at least for mothers trying to remove the stains from school uniforms.

Given the limitations and drawbacks of the system, the acme of ambition was to have a pen of one's own: not a holder to dip, but a real fountain pen. One birthday I was given what I most coveted; a marbled shiny green Conway Stewart, quite small, with a gold nib and, along its side, a little lever which you pulled out at a right-angle to the barrel, before putting the pen into a bottle of ink and slowly returning the lever to its original position to draw the ink up into the reservoir. The box it came in also held a matching propelling pencil, which struck me as terrifically stylish, especially with the pink eraser it harboured, together with spare lengths of lead: but it was the pen that meant most.

In time the Conway Stewart was succeeded by an even grander pen, a grey Parker 51 which lasted for years. It had an extra fine nib that you could only just see at the tip of the streamlined rounded barrel. Nowadays I am the happy owner of a lovely Waterman, made in Paris, black with a gold band and clip.

No one could really lament the passing of the old system, unless prone to a degree of obsessive nostalgia possibly requiring treatment, but the relatively new world of computers and the digital age has led, among other changes, to a significant shift in the relationship between mind and body. I don't mean the alarming claims that are made about the effect of computers on memory, which seems difficult to measure, or the deleterious consequences of too much screen time, which are only too easy to see, but in a way something much simpler. The pen could be seen as the outermost muscle of the mind, in a way that a screen cannot. The act of bending over the paper with pen in hand is one that can promote thoughtful consideration and focus. The resultant writing may not have any guarantee of legibility, but it does have character and is free of the spurious authority sometimes accorded to print. Well before the advent of the pseudo-science of graphology someone's handwriting was considered an element of their character, part of their identity.

But perhaps print is actually less authoritative now than it was: cut, paste, edit and delete are agents of the provisional, not of permanence. 'In the beginning was the word' is a version of authority that in the age of the image is losing its old hold on durability. Good riddance, many would say – and certainly in practical terms, who would not welcome the ability to shift and alter text as simply as is now possible? For compilers of documents, it can only be a blessed release to be freed from razor blades, Tippex, carbon paper and erasers so abrasive that they could easily fret a hole in the paper: and economising on the use of paper is another good in itself. Thanks to e-mail and texts, it is simple to put in place in, say, under an hour arrangements which before might have taken days of phone calls or weeks of correspondence. But these real transformations come at a price. E-mails and texts don't do nuance: speed of response can result in superficiality, reflex can usurp reflection. Social media display the same ambiguity, particularly in the realm of pictures. It's great to be able to send images so easily, and to take photos without the sweat and cost (environmental as well as financial) of developing and printing. No one thinks twice about taking a photo (and it's noticeable that nowadays many children seem to have a camera-ready smile to be switched on as required): anything more than breathing qualifies for a picture. All well and good, except insofar as it may run the risk of not really attending to what is in front of the lens. Capturing a face or a feature in a picture may, if we are not careful, become a way of not thinking about it, a new justification for Eliot's line in 'The Dry Salvages', 'We had the experience but missed the meaning'.

In Berlin recently, unable to find either a post office or a letter-box, I asked several people, all of whom looked baffled. Not so much, you felt, because no one had an answer to offer, but because they were amazed that anyone should be asking such a question. It reinforced what I already knew from the dwindling fortunes of the Royal Mail in England – that the age of the postal system as it has been over nearly two centuries is all but past. As with the advent of the digital age generally, there is no going back, and many of the consequent changes bring great advantages. But, again, there is a cost. Correspondence – the exchange of letters and cards with friends as well as relatives, has been a treasured source of delight over the years. Not so much those 'letters of thanks, letters from banks' mentioned in Auden's poem 'Night Mail', but certainly the 'Letters of joy from girl and boy' of the next line, and the sheer diversity celebrated later in the same poem:

Written on paper of every hue,
The pink, the violet, the white and the blue,
The chatty, the catty, the boring, the adoring,
The cold and official and the heart's outpouring, ...

Ah, 'the heart's outpouring' – in literature, where would we have been without love letters, billets doux, confessions, declarations, let alone the epistolary novel? Of course the new technology provides ample scope for alternative aids to plotting, such as the email sent to the wrong person, or finding unwelcome news on someone else's computer – and maybe in time we shall decide that emojis can stand as complete expressions of emotion. Much of this is generational: for someone of my age, at least, it is impossible not to regret the impending close of the age of letter-writing on paper, even the attendant procedures of finding the right paper or card, getting stamps, then going out to catch the post. And, as a recipient, you wait eagerly for the sound of the letter-box flipping open and the post landing with a thud.

No point in lamenting time and tide moving on, of course, but still reason enough for an affectionate celebration of what the vanishing system had to offer. From a correspondence sustained over the years, surely one of the deepest forms of loving friendship, to individual letters such as the last one I received from my father – these constitute evidence of a kind that I want to be able to hold in my hand and re-read. A letter from my father was a rarity, and his handwriting a kind of flatlining hardly punctuated at all by loops, curlicues or other clues: it had to be sent on to my mother, who wrote in her guesses between the lines. His last, written a month or so before his death, reached me in the Canary Islands, delivered to the ship on which I was returning from a teaching job in Kenya. A sky-blue air letter, of the kind that you wrote on, then folded and stuck down by licking its glued edges, it was somewhat more legible than most of his letters. He wrote that he was looking forward to retirement (he was just sixty-two) and to seeing more of us after we got back. Meanwhile, he had a request: 'Bring me some more of those damn cheap Canarias cigars'. Not significant, except in health terms, but somehow very characteristic. I could hear him saying it with a smile, in his heavily accented English, and it still makes me smile too.

*

Nowadays, if I produce my black and gold Waterman pen in public, in a shop or office, as like as not it will call forth exclamations of surprise but sometimes also of wonder – as if the sight of it could still provoke something of the same residual respect that some people retain, years later, for the poems they learnt at school.

15

Dover sole

Fish Magic

Here lies the holy fish: its fading gloss
Comes off as tacky sequins on your hand.
Nothing averts its eyes of milk and glass,
Or improves the dead sourness
Of its downturned mouth.

White meat conveyed to the white tooth,
That melts in a memory of salt,
That leaves its taste on your tongue –
But it leaps to life in a thousand
Chevrons of bone, is away
In infinite flicks of muscle,
In the only afterlife it knows,
The resurrection of numbers.

*

The mucous feel of the raw sole. And its colour, grey with a hint of green on one side, nakedly white on the other. None of the rust-marks of plaice.

No longer relevant, the miraculous ability it had to camouflage itself, almost invisible as it lay on the seabed, only its eye not taking on the hue and texture of its immediate surroundings. The slightest of bulges in the pebbly floor.

Single in its splendour, the Dover – but once I saw a whole parade of them. Not washed up on a shop counter, but filed along the forearm of Mr Albert Boggis, fishmonger, of St John's Street, Bury St Edmunds. From the back of the shop he carried them in on his skin, sheaved and symmetrical, as if they were a party trick.

Cooking a Dover sole is as simple and satisfactory as that repeated vowel sound in the two words of its name. No flour needed (please – it's a French habit that often results in the flour charring, giving the whole thing a strong by-taste): just grill it, with butter, a little salt and pepper. The perfect lunch, with a green salad and new potatoes.

And the eating of it. The flatness versus the meatiness. The pleasure of taking it apart neatly: the knife and fork please, nurse.

Then, the beautiful architecture of the skeleton, its symmetry. The wonder of such intricacy in its triple concealment – under the skin, under the delicate flesh, under the rippling surface of the sea, hidden among the light grey and green bedding of gravel.

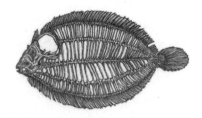

16

Sweat and guile

I t was one of the oddest things that could have happened – to be sent away from home at the age of thirteen, from Devon to a boarding school in Dorset. But because there was never any discussion of the matter, it was something that just happened, like an accident, and had to be accepted. That didn't make it much easier. I hadn't boarded before, and had no idea until I got to Sherborne how much the world of a boarding school was a matter of rules but also of rituals, all of which had to be learned, adhered to or circumvented.

The first weeks were particularly weird for any number of reasons, among them getting used to a cold shower by an open window every morning and, even worse, lavatories without doors. Also high on the list were obstacles such as the detachable stiff or semi-stiff shirt collars we had to wear, a prime instance of not making life simple when it could be so difficult. Manipulating the short collar stud at the back of the neck, and the longer one in front, was a particular skill, and if the front stud broke, as it sometimes did, you had to hope that you could either borrow one or use your tie somehow to hold everything in position, even though you felt as if you were coming apart… But the weirdest feature of the early days on this alien planet involved the boy Whitehurst. 'Boy' may not be quite accurate, as he was confidently said to be at least twenty-one. It seemed plausible. P.R. Whitehurst was improbably tall, with a gauntness about his features that suggested he had been trapped and clamped in a door early on in life. I never knew his first name and wouldn't have expected to, since it was understood that you rarely if ever spoke to those senior to you: but he was commonly known as 'Er' since, whether from genuine uncertainty or a need to play for time, that was his first utterance on any subject. He appeared more like someone in middle age than a schoolboy, rather as Cardew Robinson did in the comic *Film Fun*, but then that was also true of a number of the senior boys who, though no more than seventeen or eighteen, looked as though they would easily qualify for a place in one of those stern Victorian team photos where everyone has his arms folded, is frowning belligerently and looks the wrong side of forty.

I knew almost nothing about Whitehurst – where he lived, whether he was an only child or had siblings, what his parents did, what subjects he was studying, what his interests were. Except for a single fact, that is: Whitehurst was the house captain of fives, and this appeared to be not so much an interest as the basis of his existence. All I knew about fives, which I had never heard of before, was that it was apparently a bit like squash, only not, and that players had no such thing as a raquet to hit the ball with, only their hands in padded gloves. The ball you played with was hard and white, while a squash ball was soft and black.

Before the term was more than a few weeks old, Whitehurst took us new boys down to the fives courts – not the rather unimpressive ones by the swimming pool, but the two superior ones back-to-back and close to the nearby C.C.F. armoury. Superior being a relative term, since a fives court is a pretty basic structure. Here were four walls, beneath a sloping roof of toughened glass from which hung large lights in round metal holders, with wire guards to protect the bulbs. A painted strip of wood ran across the front wall about two feet or so above the floor: the walls themselves were surfaces of hard, smooth stone, or could have been rendered concrete. You entered the court through a small wooden door set in the back wall, and wooden stands against the outside of the back wall allowed spectators to climb up and follow the game. With these fives courts, as with most, the considerable gap between the top of the back wall and the bottom of the roof meant that they were at the mercy of the weather.

Whitehurst had with him an old Huntley & Palmers biscuit tin, which turned out to hold the necessary kit of gloves and balls. At that time gloves were either Slazengers - a deep orange in colour, which deepened to brown as they grew older; or Grasshoppers, which were white and more obviously elasticated at the wrist, giving them a slightly frilly look. Whichever make your gloves were, it was only a matter of time before the stitching came undone or the padding shifted, leaving areas which gave no protection at all and could result in considerable tenderness and bruising of the hand, especially the part of the palm just below the index finger. As to the ball, it was very slightly larger than a golf ball and not quite as frisky, though still lively enough. It was a composition ball of cotton and rubber round a cork core, with a white leather cover. This was in quarters, as a peeled orange might be, and stitched together with attractive red thread, though in later versions the joins were glued. Each ball had its own character: at its fastest when new, it might last some weeks, getting gradually slower, or it might go out of shape quite quickly, or the cover might come unstitched or unglued.

As in squash, you can only actually score when you are serving, but the game goes to 15 points rather than

9 (though 11 is possible if agreed beforehand). In most versions of the game doubles can be played, as well as singles. You serve by throwing the ball up against a corner of the front wall (the right corner if you are right-handed and, logically enough, the left if you are left-handed). The ball has to strike the front wall above the wooden bar, then the side wall, then bounce: the server then hits it back the way it has come. A good serve can be very fast and produce a satisfying *crack!* as it rockets diagonally towards the back of the court, where the receiver is waiting for it. As in general play, a return of serve can be played as a full toss (rare) or when the ball has bounced once on the floor, though it may also come off a side wall or the back wall. Again, as in squash, a boast – that is, a shot that hits one or both side walls before the front wall, or is played off the back wall, is not uncommon. The size of a fives court can vary, but those that produce the most exhilarating contests are the smaller ones, which make for faster play. There is considerable pleasure to be had in following the course of the ball onto the back wall, and then catching it at the best moment (and the timing has to be right), turning with it and whacking it at speed back to the front wall. You soon know if it's worked: if your shot is too low and hits the bar, the distinctive wooden sound will tell you.

The name 'fives' must stand for the fingers of the

hand. It's an old game, said to have been played in the angles of the flying buttresses of churches, and later developing into three distinct versions: Eton Fives, Rugby Fives and Winchester Fives. Alas! What this immediately tells you is that, in common with too many other sports, it was for a long time the province of those few whose situation and social status gave them the chance to practice it. You could argue that it was never likely to have had more than a limited following, and that this is still likely, given the cost of constructing a court. On the other hand, running costs and maintenance are low. In the second half of the twentieth century a number of existing courts were converted to squash courts, downgraded to furniture or equipment stores, or demolished altogether. Since then there have been encouraging signs of a renaissance, with more schools taking up the game including some in the state sector, the construction of new courts, and the welcome participation of women players.

The three main versions of fives differ greatly from one another, and it's probably the case that you prefer the one you learned first; in fact, you may well have experience only of that form of the game. Eton Fives courts have no back wall, a step halfway back, a ledge running round the court at about chest height, and a buttress (in imitation of Eton College Chapel) also halfway back and on the left side. Only doubles are played, and each game goes up to 12. Winchester Fives courts are a kind of halfway house between the Eton and Rugby ones, with a smaller buttress and a step but also a really high back wall. It's Rugby Fives that was – and is – played at Sherborne: the court is nothing more than a bare almost-room, with not a step or buttress or ledge in sight. That makes it somehow akin to the workings of the imagination: a latency, a potential only realised when actively in use, but then highly enjoyable.

The five-letter words that best fit fives are sweat and guile. In hot weather the sweat pours off you; in any season, the gloves in particular are impregnated with it. And the best players I've known have been absolutely full of guile. It was true of Whitehurst, whose hands seemed to materialise out of nowhere to return the ball, and even more so of Vic Marks, the England cricketer I was lucky enough to have as a partner for some time, when he and I were running the fives at Blundell's School (whose teams in those days invariably beat Sherborne). Vic, a sportsman with wonderful natural gifts, was a spin bowler, so knew all about guile. When himself a pupil at Blundell's he had been taught fives by Chris Reichwald, another outstanding sportsman and an exceptionally crafty fives player. Both of them revelled in the humour which is one of the game's chief features. In part this is because, as in squash and many other sports, you are in a battle of wits with your opponent; but much more because of the game's inbuilt character and eccentricities. Fives is not elegant, and particularly when doubles are being played, the court can seem a crowded place full of incident – plenty of pushing; appeals for obstruction; the ball sometimes striking an opponent who hasn't ducked in time; claims for lets. And then there's the weather. Unless the court is entirely indoors it can be one of the coldest places on earth. That means much noisy banging together of the gloves before the game starts, in an effort to warm the hands properly and avoid bruising. In wet weather roofs are known to leak, with the resulting puddles having to be treated with small heaps of sawdust and the floor then swept, in the hope that the dripping will have stopped. Sometimes the walls and floor stream with condensation, making the ball shoot wildly, and the floor become as dangerously slippy as an ice rink. In extreme weather rain or snow may drive into the court from the back as well as the roof, and play not be possible at all.

After playing a great deal at school, thanks to that early Whitehurst induction, I continued as an occasional player with a delightful group in Exeter until, in my fifties, my knees told me it was time to quit. By then there was no quantifying the amusement, companionship and pleasure I had had from playing the game. I'm entirely at one with the view expressed by William Hazlitt (himself a good player), writing in 1819 in *The Examiner* on the death of the Irishman John Cavanagh, the outstanding player of his time:

> It may be said that there are things of more importance than striking a ball against a wall – there are things indeed which make more noise and do as little good, such as making war and peace, making speeches, and answering them, making verses, and blotting them; making money and throwing it away. But the game of fives is what no one despises who has ever played at it. It is the finest exercise for the body, and the best relaxation for the mind.

17

Talking straight

The list of French texts set for the 1959 A Level exams included Molière's comedy of manners *Le Misanthrope*, and I shall always be grateful to my teacher, Peter Currie, for choosing it. It is a beautifully constructed play, and the kind of comedy that keeps you thinking (in my case, for some sixty years) long after the initial laughter has given way to a more reflective chuckle.

Alceste, the misanthrope of the title (and the play has a sub-title too, *The Bilious Lover*), believes that it is essential to tell the truth forthrightly about everything and in all situations. Finding himself in a world where this manifestly doesn't happen, he is in a perpetual state of rage. In a long expository opening scene which is a model of its kind, we see him from the outset furious with his friend Philinte. Invited to explain the cause of his anger, Alceste can initially only come up with the kind of reaction you might expect from a sulky teenager: 'Moi, je veux me fâcher, et ne veux pas entendre.' ('*I want* to be angry, and don't want to listen'). He is enraged, it transpires, because Philinte has flattered a virtual stranger, an apparently unforgivable crime in Alceste's eyes: 'Allez, vous devriez mourir de pure honte' ('Come on, you ought to die of pure shame'). In the face of Philinte's good-humoured suggestion that his is not a hanging offence, Alceste states his unswerving belief: 'Je veux qu'on soit sincère, et qu'en homme d'honneur / On ne lâche aucun mot qui ne parte du cœur.' ('I want people to be candid, and for no good man to impart / a single word that does not come from the heart.') But that second 'je veux...' is quickly followed by a third: 'Je veux qu'on me distingue: et pour le trancher net, /L'ami du genre human n'est point du tout mon fait.' ('I want to stand out: and, not to make the point too finely, / The friend of the human race is no friend of mine.'). This petulance begins to give the game away: not only because of the self-centred obduracy suggested by those repetitions, but also the patent absurdity of that blanket condemnation. 'Je veux qu'on me distingue' – does Alceste quite realise what he is saying? Truth-telling is to spare no one, it seems, not even the teller.

Philinte remains impressively calm under fire, putting the case for moderation – 'La parfaite raison fuit toute extrémité' ('Perfect reason knows to shun all extremes'), and reminding Alceste that his attitude hardly seems compatible with his feelings for Célimène, a young widow known for her flightiness and love of gossip. This is a point that Alceste is forced to concede, while protesting 'Mais la raison n'est pas ce qui règle l'amour' ('But it is not reason that governs love').

By the end of this opening scene, the conflict zone has been clearly defined: and the play's action goes on to test – and exploit for its comic possibilities – the feasibility of Alceste's tenets in the real world. The first challenge arrives immediately in the person of Oronte, who begins with a gush of oily flattery whose purpose soon becomes clear: he wants Alceste's opinion of a sonnet he has written. Significantly, Alceste's initial response is to decline, in terms that sound much closer to Philinte's reasonableness than his own angry edginess - 'J'ai le défaut / D'être un peu plus sincère qu'il ne faut' ('I have the fault / Of being somewhat more sincere than I ought'), and even when faced with Oronte's insistence that he really longs to have Alceste's true opinion, that is some time coming. Oronte's reading aloud of his overblown sonnet, complete with anxious self-interruptions that make clear the extent to which his vanity is engaged, is a comic highpoint. Faced with Alceste's continuing reluctance to pronounce, Oronte finds himself forced to question him as to the possible nature of the poem's faults: even then Alceste's courage seems to fail him, with his repeated denials of the negative criticisms which, Oronte speculates, may be in his mind: 'Je ne dis pas cela' ('That's not what I'm saying'), he protests no fewer than three times. Meanwhile, Philinte stokes Alceste's anger by heaping insincere praise on Oronte's effort. All of which makes it the more delicious, of course, when finally Alceste does come out with his damning opinion of the sonnet, scandalising its author.

But the most severe test of Alceste's outlook is his relationship with Célimène, already identified by Philinte as the crux of the matter. How is the purveyor of unvarnished truth to cope with the conduct of someone whose views are so alien to his own, but for whom he entertains strong feelings? In Act II we soon find out, in the first scene where they appear together. He comes straight to the point, rather in the tone of a teacher reprimanding a wayward pupil: 'Vous avez trop d'amants qu'on voit vous obséder, / Et mon cœur de cela ne peut s'accommoder.' ('You have too many suitors you're obsessed with pleasing, / And with that my heart cannot feel at ease.') At the same time, he cannot help seeking a signal from her on his own account, even though he feels quite unable to settle for her assurance that he should take encouragement from 'le bonheur de savoir que vous êtes aimé' ('the happiness of knowing you are loved').

It soon becomes apparent to the audience that

Alceste's version of love is a compound of bullying, possessiveness and his dread of rejection, each feeding on the other: not really love at all. When the arrival of the two foppish marquis Acaste and Clitandre is announced, Alceste makes to leave, but Célimène insists that he stay. Today Acaste and Clitandre (and, even more, Arsinoé, the malign prude who surfaces later in the play) would probably be enjoying a career as internet trolls: as it is, they are delighted to engage with Célimène in the character assassination of various mutual acquaintances. When Alceste is driven to protest, he calls down on himself a similar cutting assessment – woundingly, from Célimène herself:

Et ne faut-il pas bien que Monsieur contredise?
A la commune voix veut-on qu'il se réduise,
Et qu'il ne fasse pas éclater en tous lieux
L'esprit contrariant qu'il a reçu des cieux?
Le sentiment d'autrui n'est jamais pour lui plaire;
Il prend toujours en main l'opinion contraire,
Et penserait paraître un homme commun,
Si l'on voyait qu'il fût de l'avis de quelqu'un.

(And mustn't Sir insist on the opposite say?
Is there a demand for his relegation
To the general view, must he everywhere on earth
Sport the contrary spirit god-given at birth?
He never will be pleased by the views others hold,
But will always reach out for the opposite pole,

And would think himself one of the common herd,
If with another he were seen to concur.)

This is enough to make Alceste retreat smartly to the ramparts of his defensive hectoring: 'Plus on aime quelqu'un, moins il faut qu'on le flatte' ('The more you love someone, the less the need for flattery') – not a smart enough defence, though, if you take it to its logical conclusion, as Célimène is quick to point out.

Alceste and Oronte, Alceste and Célimène – but the cattiest, sharpest confrontation doesn't involve him directly at all. The acid, slow-release battle between Célimène and Arsinoé in Act III loses none of its force on re-reading: it's a wonderful comic realisation of where the play's core subject of truth can lead. Circling ever closer, the two women execute the verbal equivalent of scratching each other's eyes out. Sugar-coated with apparent concern for the other, full of sarcastic effusions, their words show how the truth can be marshalled in the interests of malice and remind us, as do the flowery circumlocutions of Acaste and Clitandre, that a play about the truth must also be about the language of truth. Is that to be the curt, ill-tempered interventions of Alceste, or the civility of Philinte and his friend Eliante, even though this may involve some compromise with social niceties? And what about the idioms of love? It is the weaponry of language that can promote hypocrisy as much as attack it, and which plays its part in throwing up a bow-wake in defence of vanity as with Acaste, or uncertainty as in the case of Alceste.

Mining all these possibilities for their comic yield, *Le Misanthrope* is beautifully balanced. The differing excesses of two of the principal male characters – Alceste's anger and Oronte's outraged vanity, involve them in an eccentric dance round the pivot of Philinte's middle ground: in the same way, the flightiness of Célimène and the malicious plotting of Arsinoé are seen against the contrasting poise and reasonableness of Eliante. For Philinte in particular, the world is as it is, and there is absolutely nothing to be gained by railing against it or trying to change human nature. It has been suggested that with his detachment and amused irony it is he who is the real misanthrope, while Alceste's fuming is the camouflage of a disappointed optimist. It is also interesting that in the final act, when Célimène is cornered and needs help, Eliante fails to come to her aid even though she is her cousin, declaring that 'je suis pour les gens qui disent leur pensée' ('I'm in favour of people who speak their mind'), which would seem to put her on the side of Alceste after all.

What is certain, in the operatic manoeuvres of the play's *dénouement*, is that leopards don't change their spots. Mortified by the wounding remarks about all of them made in a slanderous letter written by Célimène, which Acaste reads out loud, he and Clitandre do what they can to salvage their pride in the teeth of the unpleasant truth. Arsinoé offers her hand to Alceste, who refuses it and offers his own to Eliante, who promptly declares her preference for Philinte. But before that final twist Célimène has rather touchingly admitted her mistake, telling Alceste that although she cares nothing for the others he at least has the right to hate her. Predictably, while deploring his continuing affection for her as a weakness, Alceste ignores the gift horse staring him in the face: magnanimity is not a problem he suffers from. Instead, he offers her one last chance: if she will retreat from society and go with him to his 'désert', he will forgive her. I rather like the idea of Alceste stumbling into some literal Sahara, but apparently it means here his house in the country, the prospect of life away from court society being its own form of dehydration and death. Célimène's alarmed response – 'La solitude effraye une âme de vingt ans' ('Solitude is terrifying for a soul aged twenty') – seems absolutely reasonable, but is too much for Alceste, even though it comes with a tentative offer of marriage.

I used to think that, finally, it was Alceste who was the victim – both of his own shortcomings, but also of his failure to realise what it will be like for him to retire to a life of isolation. Even more than the other characters, he needs people around him: and he does not seem to be aware of the affection that others retain for him despite his laughable failings, his biliousness and his propensity for unwarranted indignation. As an emotion, anger actually demands an audience if it is to be anything more than pathological. And when all is said and done, his demand for truthfulness and candour in people's dealings with one another is not altogether unworthy. As Eliante says of him in Act IV:

> Et la sincérité dont son âme se pique
> A quelque chose en soi de noble et d'héroïque

> (And sincerity, his soul's nervous tic,
> Has something inherently noble and heroic)

But what of Célimène? Throughout the play there is a crescendo of demands that she declare herself for one or other of her suitors. The showdown of the final scene, with her abject confession in public, is nothing better than an ambush, suggesting that in the end she more than anyone is a victim of the truth.

18

Kindly lights

Long before we were old enough to know how reactionary his views were on almost every subject, my sister and I immersed ourselves in the ten volumes of Arthur Mee's *Children's Encyclopædia*, which our mother had managed to acquire second-hand, assuming that something calling itself an encyclopædia could be relied upon to be objective and factual. The original publication was in serial form, and a number of entries had headings that were repeated from one volume to the next, such as the short lessons relaying the French for such timeless phrases as 'The maid helped the boys to pack the large trunk with their toys', or the series headed 'Things to do on a rainy afternoon', which included such excitements as 'How to knock over a brick upon a table'. This and other activities may well have been intended to keep children's hands in the right place: there was to be no nonsense, whatever the weather, witness the smudgy black and white photos of Greek or Roman gods and heroes (of which there were quite a few) with their genitalia airbrushed out. No exception was made for Cupid.

Mr Mee was absolutely certain of who was who when it came to separating the sheep from the goats. Among his *bêtes noires* were jazz bands (often *noirs*, of course) and gin, while batting for virtue were such as Jack Cornwall V.C. and David Livingstone, with Joan of Arc ('the stainless maid of France') allowed to join the team even though she was a foreigner, as a rule-proving exception. Another of the elect was Grace Darling, the lighthouse keeper's daughter famous for going to the aid of stricken mariners. A large illustration showed her rowing through mountainous seas, impervious to danger and intent on her gallant mission to rescue sailors from the shipwrecked vessel *Forfarshire*.

It was this picture, working with the enthusiasm I was already developing for the sea and boats, which first got me interested in lighthouses. They seemed in themselves such heroic structures, precariously located on minimal ledges of dark rock, and manned by the equally heroic figure of the lighthouse keeper, isolated as he was and often cut off from the world by gales and storms. It was a frequent habit of cinema newsreels at Christmas time to screen shots of lighthouse keepers: they were seen tucking into goodies sent them by well-wishers wanting to bring a little seasonal cheer to these noble guardians of the light.

Their shape and size give lighthouses an obvious emblematic value, though Mr Mee might not have approved of the way they rear up. With its image of a light shining in the midst of danger and darkness, it's not surprising that the lighthouse has been adopted by many charities and churches as their symbol. There are memorable instances, too, of lighthouses as the subject of paintings: among my favourites are Edward Hopper's picture of the lighthouse at Two Lights, in Maine (a subject he returned to several times), and the watercolour by Eric Ravilious of the lighthouse at Beachy Head. He also did a painting from the interior of the old Beachy Head lighthouse, Belle Tout, a view looking out from the lantern room. For sheer drama, though, it would be hard to match Turner's painting of the Bell Rock Lighthouse, off the Angus coast, a picture commissioned by the designer and builder Robert Stevenson as a frontispiece for his *Account of the Bell Rock Lighthouse.*

It was two of Stevenson's sons, David and Thomas, who as civil engineers were responsible for the construction of some thirty lighthouses on and around the coasts of Scotland. A typical Stevenson lighthouse has a square or quadrilateral building at its base, housing stores and equipment and providing accommodation: and from the middle of this cluster, or very close to it, rises the tower itself. This is the design of the lighthouse they built on the Orcadian island of Auskerry in 1866. Apart from the steading at the other end of the island, it's the island's only building, if you discount a few outhouses and a ruined chapel.

You won't find Auskerry on many maps: if you do, it is likely to be shown as a miniscule tear-drop on the eastern periphery of the Orkneys, three miles south of Stronsay. For more than thirty-five years it has been the home of our friends Simon and Teresa Brogan, who home educated their sons Rory, Owen and Hamish on the island up to the age of fourteen. All three boys have taken 'Auskerry' as their surname. Now that they have grown up and moved away, Simon and Teresa are the island's only inhabitants, along with a large flock of seaweed-eating North Ronaldsay sheep, 'Rollies', one of just two remaining flocks in the Orkneys.

The rich immanence of the place is very hard to capture. Each of its features might be marked on a child's map of an island promising adventure or treasure – a standing stone; a ruined medieval chapel where stormy petrels gather at night, taking off in a clamour of wingbeats and fuss; the skeleton of a beached whale; the remains of the *Hastings County,* a Norwegian cargo ship wrecked in thick fog within 1,000 metres of the lighthouse in 1926, breaking in half. From its resting-place on the rocks, two remnants of derricks or masts, each in the shape of the letter Y, still aim their questions at the sky. And then there is the lighthouse itself, automated in 1961.

This is no make-believe island: even though the islanders are not completely self-sufficient, with monthly provisioning by boat from Kirkwall fifteen miles to the west (and the passage only possible when the weather allows), life on Auskerry is demanding. To visitors used to taking such things as water and electricity for granted, there are salutary reminders that both are finite resources. Three small wind turbines and four solar panels provide most of the power: water comes from a spring that emerges from a cliff face about halfway along the island from the steading. There are no roads, and the only means of transport is a doughty tractor that, with its wooden trailer, bucks and bangs over ground that is particularly stony around field gates.

There is always something that needs doing: sheep to round up, shear or tend; the chemical toilet to empty;

a roof to repair or replace; fences to mend; peat to cut; water to fetch from the spring; the vegetables in the small garden to encourage. Then there is the business built up by Teresa over the years, producing from the fleeces of the Rollies blankets, rugs, fleece and yarn, by methods as natural and sustainable as possible, with the sheep sheared by hand. Again, it's hard work, but rewarding – and thanks to the internet Teresa has been able steadily to develop a market for her products.

During their time on Auskerry, Simon and Teresa have done much to develop the steading, too. The original one-room stone bothy has become a four-bedroomed house, to the great benefit of visiting friends, who are readily welcomed, and all the more if they can lend a hand. Auskerry has its own generous version of hospitality.

Still there is something elusive about the place, which makes it more than the sum of its parts. And what parts! You want sea-life? Try dolphins, porpoises, seals and the occasional whale for a start. You can be amongst many of these creatures at close quarters, when Simon takes you out in his Orkney Longliner with its outboard. This is straight back to a child's adventure: the seals mildly curious about our presence but scarcely bothered, some out on the rocks, others bobbing nearby, their heads swivelling occasionally like raised periscopes; the huge floating rafts of greylag geese; the boat nosing into small coves and caves hollowed out by the tides at the foot of the cliffs.

As for birds, here come oystercatchers, terns, puffins, razorbills, guillemots common and black, fulmars, dippers and moorhens as well as those stormy petrels up by the chapel. With the terns, you'd better be ready to duck as they may dive-bomb you, especially if you are walking close to their nests on the ground.

The flora is every bit as rich – the yellow marsh irises, the tiny gold flowers of the tormentils, silverleaf, Yorkshire fog and other grasses. Above and beyond all that, there is the purity of salt and ozone, the clarity of the air which, along with sunny weather, always has the character of some extra endowment. And then, on the sea, broad strips of silver light alternating with darker ones plucked at by the breeze: sunrise as an orange dome, lit from within, that has alighted on the sea. At sunset, bars of fiery light lie across the molten waters, before the darkness comes on, often as a soft half-light.

Most elusive of all, there is the whole atmosphere of the island and its rhythms, in alliance with those of the moon and the tides, as well as weather which can manifest itself in long periods of high winds and rain, or envelop the island in muffling fog, or bestow sunlight upon it. There is, too, a slowing of time, but with a quickening intensity: and between bird cries and the bleating of the sheep, a silence that their voices magnify. Here on the island superstructure has no place.

The lighthouse plays its part in all this. At the opposite end of the island from the steading, the top of its thirty-four metre tower is just visible, peering over the rising ground at the island's centre. At night the regular sweep of its beam, so much more powerful than the loom of other lights below the horizon, casts a spell of its own. It's one of my abiding images of Auskerry: but so too is the woven oval of the snipe's nest discovered half hidden in long grass close to the peat stack, for what it says of survival, persistence, a home islanded on an island. One day it held two eggs, green speckled with brown: the next, four.

*

David and Thomas Stevenson were sons of Robert the builder of lighthouses. Thomas married Maggie Balfour. Their son, Robert Louis Stevenson, caused his parents great disappointment by not following in the family footsteps, becoming a writer instead.

From the Lighthouse

At the rough-cut edge
of the land, a megaphone
of light, naked
as distress itself,
blares sideways across
the abraded acres of the sea.

If this were a book, you'd call it
one with a preface and afterword
and a bright ribbon
to mark your progress
from the underworld of the past
to the thin air of the future.

19

The secret orchard

I have no memory of the first time I lay in an orchard, though I've been told about it often enough. My sister and I had been parked in a big double pram beneath a tree in the orchard, at the small farm our parents had a few miles west of Exeter. Somehow, by dint of fidgeting or rocking, we managed to free the pram from the stone placed under one of its wheels to prevent it running away. It bumped and careered down the slope, gathering speed as it went. Miraculously it is said to have avoided other trees and obstacles, and to have come finally to rest where the ground levelled out, close to an open gateway leading onto the lane.

Much later, on the relatively rare occasions that we went up to London, always by train, a few miles out of Exeter we would steam past the magnificent Whiteways cider orchards on the southern side of the track. Crazy with the foam of blossom in spring, they were even better in the autumn, when the trees seemed impossibly weighed down by their profusion of red fruit.

I'm not sure that either of these youthful experiences quite explains the fascination I feel for orchards. In one place or another, they kept on waving at me as I grew up, sometimes from unexpected locations. There an orchard was, for instance, in Browning's 'Home Thoughts from Abroad', which we had to learn at school, complete with a chaffinch singing on a bough. Less likely was its recurrence when, as a sixth former, I took part in a performance of *Julius Caesar*: not only was the conspiracy against Caesar hatched in Brutus's orchard at night, but in the next act there was Mark Antony (played on this occasion by Richard Eyre, later Director of the National Theatre) reading Caesar's will to the crowd:

> Moreover, he hath left you all his walks,
> His private arbours, and new-planted orchards,
> On this side Tiber, he hath left them you,
> And to your heirs forever; common pleasures,
> To walk abroad and recreate yourselves.

The mention of orchards in the context of political assassination seems vivid but a bit incongruous – perhaps that is because I have always thought of orchards as essentially domestic in height and extent, in keeping with the accepted definition of a traditional orchard as having at least five trees, with them only having to be tall enough to allow cattle to graze under their branches.

For me, there is more to it than that. Of course the fruits of the orchard – which might be damsons, pears, plums or even nuts, as well as apples, are rewarding in their own right, and for children most of all when won by scrumping, with its added savour of transgression and risk, let alone the Tree of Knowledge. However the fruit comes to hand, there is something magical about being able to pluck it straight from the tree. It's a magic that extends to the whole area of the orchard, the idea of it. Neither a garden, quite, nor a field, it might lead on from one and look out to the other, an interspace distinct from both. This is true even of commercial orchards, with their long straight rows separated by broad strips of grass, but those that appeal to me most are smaller, less open and probably older. They can look rather more broken down, with the space between the trees patrolled by a few peevish chickens rootling among fallen branches – and the trees themselves contorted and gnarled, with a dusting of grey-green lichen.

I've always been interested, too, in paintings of orchards, such as those produced so prolifically by van Gogh in Arles, in the spring of 1888. As you might expect, he gives us the torqued trunks and branches of the trees, but many of these pictures celebrate first and foremost the white or pink blossom shooting skyward, often with an expansiveness which is also to be found, in a somewhat calmer mode, in Camille Pissarro's depictions of orchards further north, at Pontoise and Eragny.

Some of van Gogh's work shows groves rather than orchards (olives rather than apples) and perhaps it's that word, with its undertone of the sacred, which indicates better what I feel. I don't quite mean the Druidic or other ancient folklore associated with such places, and still there in the form of wassailing and other orchard ceremonies, but some richness inherent in the atmosphere. Something of it comes across in Samuel Palmer's painting known as *The Magic Apple Tree* (so named by his son Alfred Herbert, not Palmer himself), even if the tree isn't obviously within the confines of an orchard (though it could be at the periphery of one). In this fire-burst of colour, the flare of the apples is one with the fields in the background. They could be about to become an avalanche, it seems, to race downhill and wash over the church spire already half submerged at the centre of the picture. It's almost as if the whole scene has been conjured by the pipe-playing of the shepherd seated close to his flock in the foreground. 'Magic' may not have been the painter's own title, but it's not a bad word to describe the spirit the picture conveys.

If such depictions of fruitfulness are one element in

my love of orchards, another could be represented by a still, starry night in Jordan in 1962, when I and my two travelling companions were sleeping by the road, in the open. To our surprise and, initially, our alarm, a figure loomed out of the darkness from the other side of the road. Maybe he was coming to see who had arrived at the bottom of his garden, or else just taking the night air. He greeted us warmly, inviting us to come and have coffee with him, and told us to feel free to help ourselves from the fruit trees in his garden as we walked up to the house. This felt magical too, not least as an instance of hospitality which left us grateful, but also with an increased awareness of how closed our own culture could be, when it comes to welcoming strangers. There was, too, a rich and strangely unreal pleasure just in walking through the garden.

An orchard is a welcoming shelter not only for birds, insects and other creatures, but humans as well. It can offer solitude, or at least apartness and, for reasons I still don't fully understand, to be in one always engenders a real excitement in me. I want more than anything else to sleep alone under the trees, to be able to look up at the immensity of the sky through the fretted baffles of the branches. Something of that feeling is caught in the opening lines of Auden's poem 'A Summer Night', where 'Out on the lawn I lie in bed, / Vega conspicuous overhead / In the windless nights of June'. It even occurs to me, not at all in a morbid way, that an orchard would be a great place in which to be buried – for it to be, in that vivid phrase, a 'bone orchard'.

There has been no shortage of poets who write about orchards, from Rumi – 'In the orchard and rose garden I long to see your face' (in 'The Agony and Ecstasy of Divine Discontent'), to Wordsworth in 'The Green Linnet', though it may now read as far too pat ('In this sequestered nook how sweet / To sit upon my orchard-seat / And birds and flowers once more to greet'), to Robert Frost's 'A Prayer in Spring', with its imprecation 'Oh, give us pleasure in the orchard white, / Like nothing else by day, like ghosts by night' – but mostly these are references which make assumptions about the axiomatic poetry of the orchard rather than bringing it to life in any detail. In this quite general referential vein, as so often it's Emily Dickinson who, for me, comes closest:

> Some keep the Sabbath going to church,
> I keep it staying at home,
> with a bobolink for a chorister,
> and an orchard for a dome.

In these lines she captures something near to the sacred sense of an orchard, its potency as an alternative form of worship. What is still left, though, is what I feel most strongly of all, and most enjoy when in an orchard – the hiddenness of it, the light enclosure of a mystery not to be explained by looking back to the house, or out across open country.

20

Timepieces and tongues

The long-case clock that stands in the hall at home is impressively tall, about seven feet. It is late eighteenth century, with a fine mahogany case, and came down to me from my mother. Painted onto a ratchet-wheel above the face are two more faces – large circular moons, ruddy-cheeked, one on the verge of smiling, the other with a single tear-drop on its cheek. The ratchet turns in time with the phases of the moon, and is pretty accurate: and there is also a much smaller disk which shows the date. The clock has a winder a bit like the handle of an old coffee grinder: once a week the very heavy brass cylinders inside the case have to be hoisted, with a fine ticking noise as they go up, interspersed with the occasional arthritic squeak.

When I inherited the clock I reactivated the chimes (which sound a single note, the number appropriate for the hour). They were much less impressive and resonant than I remembered, more like a counter-tenor than a bass, but still loud enough to be heard in my study two floors up. There, in a drawer, is the slim silver pocket watch given to me by my father on one of his rare visits, with the explanation that it was always handed on to the eldest son in each generation. Smooth as a seashore pebble, it has the black figures 1 to 12 marching round the face, punctuated between 5 and 7 by a very small dial showing the seconds. But it also has, in a ring outside the black numbers, the figures 13 to 24 in red. Its hands, slim, black and the hour hand with a slight bulge towards its point, have a slightly iridescent sheen. The sound of the tick is so light that you have to hold the watch up to your ear to be sure it's going.

These two timepieces, so different from one another, nonetheless remind me of the decade my parents had together and make me think of what each of them brought to the marriage, as well as their very different subsequent lives which, for my father, included another child, my half-sister Amata, with his second wife Dolores. My mother re-married happily after more than a quarter of a century on her own. And I think of my father dying at the age of sixty-two, my mother (three years his junior) living to be eighty-nine; his body buried in West Somerset, her ashes in a Berkshire churchyard.

Goethe was sure about the gifts he inherited from his parents:

Vom Vater hab' ich die Statur
Des Lebens ernstes Führen,
Vom Mutterchen die Frohnatur
Und Lust zu fabulieren.

In Michael Hamburger's translation:

My build from Father I inherit,
His neat and serious ways;
Combined with Mother's cheerful spirit,
Her love of telling stories.

With my own parents, I find it hard to feel so certain of the genetic inheritance, and the difficulty is compounded by the fact that I saw my father so rarely. My mother certainly had 'die Frohnatur', and I hope something of that has come through to me: and maybe something of my father's outlook has found a furtherance by seguing from paint to print. Who knows? I was made to ponder the point a few years ago when I was doing a reading at a Bath bookshop. At the end, a woman came up to me and apologised for not being at the reading. This completely foxed me, since there she plainly was. She explained that she had a back problem which wouldn't have made it easy for her to sit through the event. She had sat outside in her car, and here she was now because she had a letter to give me from her father, Christopher Cook, a colleague of my father's at the Art School in Burton-on-Trent, his last employment.

Mr Cook's letter told me, *inter alia*, that he had seen several of my collections of poems, and noticed a couple of them had Paul Klee paintings on the front cover. Did I realise that my father had been taught by Klee at the Bauhaus in Dessau, and possibly also by Kandinsky? This I found astonishing: it also made me regret even more that contact with my father had been so infrequent. It was tantalising to think that the name of Klee had never passed between us, let alone any discussion of his work. But it also left me wondering whether such common ground could be inherited from one generation to the next, or was purely coincidental as surely it must have been.

The differences in my parents' experience of life was obvious enough: my mother brought up in a solidly middle class London family, my father trying to make a go of being an artist, having left Germany in the 1930s. Those differences were no doubt enriching for me and my sister, but I also like to think about what our parents had in common. They both loved travel, food, the delights of simple journeying and of the languages they had between them. If my mother's German and French were not always grammatical, they were spoken with obvious relish: if my father's English retained a pronounced German accent to the end of his life, he was still fluent.

*

'Of course you belong to *us* too', a German cousin wrote to me a few years ago. In a sense she was right, of course, and I am genuinely grateful for the overview of more than one territory, so to speak, even if the combined effect of my parents' divorce and my father's relatively early death has made the whole notion seem rather attenuated. So too did my father's change of name by deed poll, which (and rather irritatingly because it seems so corny) would unwittingly bundle up together my love of the sea and my surname.

Like many people, I feel split between belonging and not belonging, an ambivalence expressed in a restlessness that on the one hand has me reaching home at the end of a journey sooner than expected, and on the other feeling real excitement at the prospect of a journey ahead and its planning. 'Belonging', with the ache of longing built into it; 'be', with its undertone of static establishment; the German 'Sehnsucht', with all its literary associations. The way the sound of it sighs at you with its own longing; and the unhealthy connotations of 'Sucht', 'addiction'. It's tempting to take refuge in Czesław Miłosz's assertion that 'language is the only homeland'.

*

E PERICOLOSO SPORGERSI

NE PAS SE PENCHER AU DEHORS

NICHT HINAUSLEHNEN

IT IS DANGEROUS TO LEAN OUT

I must have been ten when I first saw this notice, on a small metal plate screwed above a train carriage window. It fascinated me – how could languages be so disparate? Not only did the warning sound quite different in each of the four languages (the dramatic allure of the Italian, the much softer caress of the French, the peremptory snap of the German, the English that I heard in my head as a typical instance of Received Pronunciation in all its official formality), they also looked different: only two words in German, but three in Italian, six in French and English.

I don't want to suggest that this was some sort of railway epiphany: but I do think of it as conveying a very particular kind of excitement. To be able to communicate and read in French and German (and, up to a point, Italian) has been of great importance to me – magnified, no doubt, by my father's origins, but important and hugely enjoyable in its own right. To have access to those languages, as well as their literature, has been an extraordinary enrichment, one that I can only properly measure when I find myself in a country where I *don't* speak the language. It has also encouraged a curiosity in the derivations of words. Just to keep to French, how can it be, for instance, that our word 'pedigree' comes from 'pied de grue', a crane's foot? Why is a particular kind of Parisian fanlight known as a 'vasistas'? What is the English word, pronounced *à la française*, that accounts for 'la redingote'? And on the same tack, what about 'le boulingrin'?

The impulse that makes me want to celebrate the diversity and individuality of languages also makes it impossible for me not to mention the really alarming decline in language learning in Britain. Apparently too many students consider languages to be 'hard', and so are put off. Perhaps the near-dominance of English in the world of computers and algorithms plays a part, along with the tendency for many English people (I'm not sure it is true of the Scots, the Welsh or the Irish) to suffer a crippling self-consciousness when called upon to speak another language. For all that, in an age that prizes 'employability' as a criterion for educational choices, you'd think it would be clear that the acquisition of a foreign language could only be advantageous. The situation is not improved by the toxic fog of populism that has rolled in to narrow our view of the world and our place in it. As Wittgenstein pointed out, 'Die Grenzen meiner Sprache bedeuten die Grenzen meiner Welt' – 'The limits of my language denote the limits of my world.'

21

The smoke-tree

Something zigzag in its branchwork
and the crown – flat, broad,
suggest China,

an overhang

above steep water

The leaves are tender, shaped
like small oval fans –
the sap, when

it oozes, has

an odd, medicinal smell

In summer the panicles, sketchy,
faintly purple, papery
as a wasps' nest,

fall and

bowl into corners

Autumn is the most exotic –
it flames through scarlet, crimson
to murrey, bright
                              as the gift
of a late insight

Coda

B en Jonson, in a poem remembering his son who died at the age of seven, imagined the boy in his grave describing himself as 'Ben Jonson his best piece of poetry'. I have been so fortunate as to have four children: Matthew and Erica in my marriage to Teresa, our twins Grace and Rose with my second wife, Helen. Though I said at the outset that this is not a familial memoir, since it is celebratory it seems entirely right to round to them.

At the outset…that was B.C., before the pandemic coronavirus had struck. It's one thing to write in the perspectives of a lifetime, another to look back from the throes of a crisis, when Before Coronavirus has swung to Coronavirus Era. To do so enlarges the distance between now and then, imparting new value to much that has been taken for granted. It can also act as a corrective – for instance, by showing that when it comes to overcoming the isolation imposed by being locked down, the internet and social media have an important part to play.

In *The Prophet*, the Lebanese poet Kahlil Gibran imagined children as 'living arrows' their parents have fired into the future. I hope that, whatever their trajectory and however they come to earth my children, when they look back, will feel something of what Auden expressed in a single line in his last collection, *Thank You, Fog* (1974), in the poem 'Lullaby'. I used to think of it as a slightly clunky reworking of the couplet with which he ended his poem of thirty-five years earlier in memory of Yeats. There he had written, mellifluously, 'In the prison of his days / Teach the free man how to praise'. The line from the later poem retains the four beats as well as the sense of a heartfelt injunction, and I've grown to like it a lot:

Let your last thinks all be thanks.

Anchor

Hope plucked
From the misty mud
All its paid out
Scope is hauled
To the bitter end.

A blessing, an icon,
It rises to light
Through bubbled pressures
And the fish flat
As pressed flowers.

Firstling of
The imagination,
Already it drifts
Free beneath
The boat going on.

Great grey hook
Even when landed
On deck it keeps
The look of clear,
Ancient depths.

Lastage of
The imagination,
Chained to the live
Hull of history
It holds fast.